FROM SHAKESPEARE
TO POPE

London: C. J. CLAY AND SON,
CAMBRIDGE UNIVERSITY PRESS WAREHOUSE,
AVE MARIA LANE.

Cambridge: DEIGHTON, BELL AND CO.
Leipzig: F. A. BROCKHAUS.

FROM SHAKESPEARE

TO POPE

AN INQUIRY INTO

THE CAUSES AND PHENOMENA OF THE RISE

OF CLASSICAL POETRY IN ENGLAND

BY

EDMUND GOSSE

CLARK LECTURER ON ENGLISH LITERATURE AT THE
UNIVERSITY OF CAMBRIDGE

CAMBRIDGE
AT THE UNIVERSITY PRESS
1885

KRAUS REPRINT CO.
New York
1968

Cambridge:
PRINTED BY C. J. CLAY, M.A. AND SON,
AT THE UNIVERSITY PRESS.

L.C. Catalog Card Number 11-21320

First published 1885
Reprinted by permission of the Cambridge University Press
KRAUS REPRINT CO.
A U.S. Division of Kraus-Thomson Organization Limited

Printed in Germany

PREFACE.

THE following chapters were written in the form of lectures, and were first delivered to members of the University of Cambridge, in the Hall of Trinity College, during Michaelmas Term last year. They formed my inaugural course as Clark Lecturer. In the month of December I read them at the Lowell Institute in Boston, and during the same winter, in whole, or in part, before other academic audiences in America, before the Johns Hopkins University in Baltimore, in New York, before Yale College, Connecticut, and elsewhere.

It has been no small advantage to me that among the distinguished listeners to whom I have had the honour of reading these pages there have been more than a few whose special studies have rendered them particularly acute in criticising the links of my argument. In consequence of such criticism, I have been able profitably to revise the work, to add evidence where it seemed wanting, to remove rash statements and to remould ambiguous sentences. Above all, I have given a great deal of care to the accumulation, in the form of notes and appendices, of historical and critical data of a kind too particular for the purposes of a lecture, but not, I hope, without genuine importance to the student of the history of literature. In an enquiry of this nature, exact evidence, even of a minute kind, outweighs in importance any expression of mere critical opinion. The friendly criticism of which I have spoken has not, however, shaken me in the slightest degree with regard to my central idea. On the contrary, the effect of minute controversy has merely been to strengthen on every side my conviction that the theory which I have here laid down for the first time is substantially the true one, and that the opinion hitherto received regarding the sources of the classical school in our poetry is erroneous. I think I may at least claim, from the critic who is inclined to reject my views, a careful consideration of the arguments and evidence upon which they are founded.

It would be impossible for me to speak too warmly of the kindness which my friend Professor Samuel R. Gardiner has shown me in allowing me to see and use the unfinished MS. of the forthcoming volume of his *History*, and in leading me to MS. sources of seventeenth-century information. It is wholly owing to his generosity that I have been enabled, in the second chapter of this volume, to give an account of Waller's Plot which is much more complete and accurate than any hitherto published. Prof. Gardiner's volume, for which students of the Caroline period can hardly command their impatience, will not, I am sorry to say, be in our possession for some years.

TRIN. COLL., CAMBRIDGE.
May, 1885.

TO W. D. HOWELLS.

The humming-bird in June
Sits, like a jewel, on your taut clothes-line,
And greets Charles River broad and opaline,
Till wanes September's honeysuckle moon
Too soon;

And then—away he goes,
A flash of ruby on the southward air,
And comes no more, though still the straits are fair,
Where misty Cambridge from the Beacon shows
Pale rose;

But leaves a plume behind,—
A little plume you fold into a book,
On which one day if you should chance to look,
Your tiny friend would rise, thro' storm and wind,
To mind.

The fluted conchs that came
Long since in Salem merchant-ships to town,
With polished porcelain lips and ridges brown,
Faint perfumed from the isles of eastern name
A-flame,—

To W. D. Howells.

These still, if shaken, give
From their deep hearts a murmur of the dome
Where once their soft inhabitants could roam,—
Sonorous seas where Indian monsters thrive
And strive;

Their owners all are dead;
The mighty ships that brought them rot on shore;
Yet still that murmur lingers at their core,
And fancy's light across their tropic bed
Is shed.

I, less than bird or shell,
More volatile, more fragile far than these,
Lighting an hour by these New England seas,
Leave here my plume, my echo,—where it fell
To dwell;

You shook it from my wing!
You dived to lift it from my glimmering deeps!
Now, wakened by your voice no more, it sleeps
And grows less mine than yours; here let it cling
And sing;

Then, when at dusk you spy
The noiseless phantom-schooners warping down
To load in mouldering wharves of Boston town,
Turn sometimes to your lamp-lit shelves, where I
Shall lie.

   302 BEACON STREET, BOSTON.
    Dec. 1884.

CONTENTS.

	PAGE
PREFACE	v
DEDICATION	ix
POETRY AT THE DEATH OF SHAKESPEARE	3
WALLER AND SACHARISSA	45
THE EXILES	95
DAVENANT AND COWLEY	137
THE REACTION	181
THE RESTORATION	225
APPENDICES	
I. Sidney Godolphin and Sandys	269
II. Denham's Essay on Translated Verse	272
III. Waller's Address to the Queen	275
IV. The Preface to Waller's Posthumous Poems, 1690	278
INDEX	285

POETRY AT THE DEATH OF SHAKESPEARE.

POETRY AT THE DEATH OF SHAKESPEARE.

THE time seems to have arrived at last, when we may contemplate without passion that precise, mundane, and rhetorical order of poetry which is mainly identified in our minds with the names and practice of Dryden, of Pope, and of Johnson. The school of writers who cultivated this order—and those who emphasise their faults admit that they did institute a school—have commonly been described as the classical, because their early leaders claimed to emulate and restore the grace and precision of the poets of antiquity, to write in English as Horace and Ovid were then supposed to have written in Latin,—that is to say, with a polished and eclectic elegance[1]. The prestige of these

---

[1] *Horace* will our superfluous Branches prune,
Give us new rules, and set our Harp in tune,
Direct us how to back the winged Horse,
Favour his flight and moderate his force.
  Waller *to Roscommon*, 1684.

classical versemen was first attacked, in the middle of the eighteenth century, by Gray and Chatterton; and their influence received blow upon blow until the close of the century, when the efflorescence of the naturalistic poets, first from within, as in Crabbe, and then much more decisively from without, as in Wordsworth and Coleridge, destroyed it altogether.

To the first and second generation after this revolution in taste, the classical species of poetry seemed no poetry at all. Dryden and Pope, who had been enthroned so long in secure promise of immortality, felt their shrines shaken as by an earthquake. It became the fashion to say that these men were no poets at all, and Keats, in a curious passage of his youth, made himself the daring spokesman of this heresy.

> "Yes, a schism
> Nurtured by foppery and barbarism
> Made great Apollo blush for this his land.
> Men were thought wise who could not understand
> His glories; with a puling infant's force
> They sway'd about upon a rocking-horse,
> And thought it Pegasus. Ah, dismal-soul'd!
> The winds of heaven blew, the ocean roll'd
> Its gathering waves—ye felt it not. The blue
> Bared its eternal bosom, and the dew
> Of summer night collected still to make
> The morning precious: Beauty was awake!

Why were ye not awake? But ye were dead
To things ye knew not of,—were closely wed
To musty laws lined out with wretched rule
And compass vile; so that ye taught a school
Of dolts to smooth, inlay, and clip, and fit,
Till, like the certain wands of Jacob's wit,
Their verses tallied. Easy was the task:
A thousand handicraftsmen wore the mask
Of Poesy. Ill-fated, impious race!
That blasphemed the bright Lyrist to his face,
And did not know it,—no, they went about,
Holding a poor, decrepit standard out,
Mark'd with most flimsy mottoes, and in large
The name of one Boileau[1]!"

In these lines Keats has so admirably summed up the convictions of the first half of the present century with regard to the classical poetry, that I need make little comment upon them, further than to point out that with the tact of a great writer he has contrived to condemn the practice he is attacking, no less by the form in which he clothes his ideas, than by the ideas themselves. The passage I have just quoted does not merely satirize the poetry which is presently coming under our consideration, but it is written in extreme formal opposition to it:—

---

[1] From *Sleep and Poetry*, ll. 181—206, published in the *Poems* of 1817.

> "The blue
> Bared its eternal bosom, and the dew
> Of summer night collected still to make
> The morning precious:"

That sentence is a cluster of what the French call *enjambments,* stridings-over; although we have so much of the thing in our literature, we have no word for it in English. It has been proposed to pronounce the French word as though it were English, enjambments, but this is hideous. My friend, Mr Austin Dobson, has proposed to me the term *overflow*[1] for these verses in which the sense is not concluded at the end of one line or of one couplet, but straggles on, at its own free will, until it naturally closes; and I propose to adopt it throughout this inquiry, as equivalent to the *vers enjambé* of the French. In its simplest definition, then, the formular difference between the two classes or orders of English poetry is, that the romantic class is of a loose and elastic kind, full of these successive overflows, while the classical is closely confined to the use of distich, that is to say, of regular couplets, within the bounds of each of which the sense is rigidly confined.

[1] Milton describes the same peculiarity in *The Verse* (*Paradise Lost*, fifth title-page) as "the sense variously drawn out from one verse into another."

It will now be well to show the distinction between these two orders by examples. The passage just quoted from Keats will serve us very well as a specimen of the romantic order. While the wayward music of it is still in our ears, I will contrast it with a few lines from Dryden:—

> "All human things are subject to decay,
> And, when Fate summons, monarchs must obey.
> This Flecknoe found, who, like Augustus, young
> Was called to empire, and had governed long,
> In prose and verse was owned, without dispute,
> Through all the realms of Nonsense, absolute.
> This aged prince, now flourishing in peace
> And blest with issue of a large increase,
> Worn out with business, did at length debate
> To settle the succession of the state;
> And, pondering which of all his sons was fit
> To reign and wage immortal war with wit,
> Cried, ''Tis resolved, for Nature pleads that he
> Should only rule who most resembles me[1].'"

The temper in which these two writers, Dryden and Keats, are here displayed, is almost identical. I have selected the second piece, because, like the first, it breathes indignation against the mediocrity of poetasters. Our ears none the less instruct us in a moment that here we have two brilliant artists whose methods, whose ambitions, whose

---

[1] *Mac-Flecknoe* (1682), ll. 1—14.

whole conception of style, are at the poles of contrast. Briefly, then, it may be said that each of the manners thus exemplified has been twice in the ascendant in English poetry. The classical, or precise, when poetry first began to be written in modern English; the romantic, when poetry revived under the Tudor monarchs; the classical again from the English Commonwealth to the French Revolution; the romantic again ever since.

The subject of our present investigation is confined to the phenomena and history of the second of these changes, that which succeeded the career of Shakespeare, and led to a new fashion which culminated in the art of Pope. That this change occurred is obvious to everybody, but the causes that led to it are so obscure, and even the history of it has hitherto been so little studied, that the inquiry we are about to pursue may be said to be practically a novel one. In undertaking it we are confronted by the difficulty which a traveller encounters in attempting minutely to survey a passage of country, part of which is flat and part is hilly. From a distance nothing seems easier than to distinguish between plain and acclivity, but when we are on the spot we find ourselves baffled, for these melt into one. It is because we have again retired to a distance from the scene of our survey that the time seems to me to have arrived for a just consideration of the classical school. We can now contemplate in a calm perspective what was too near for the generation of Keats to observe without the injustice of foreshortening.

I have hitherto spoken only of the formal character of the change which took place in English poetry towards the middle of the seventeenth century, and not of its ethicàl or essential character; because poetry is an art, and must be regarded primarily from an artistic and not from a philosophical point of view. To fail to acknowledge this to be a postulate, is to fall into an error such as a critic of music would make, although a less serious one, if he gave attention to the emotional sentiments awakened in the hearer by a performance, in priority to the science of the harmonical and melodious sounds of which that performance was the executive production. I must therefore dwell a moment longer on the formal character of the change, and beg my readers to consider the marvel of a nation that was free to use in any combination all the endless varieties of iambic and trochaic movement (for the dactylic and anapæstic[1]

---

[1] I purposely take no note here of the experiments in tumbling rimeless measure made by certain Elizabethans. These were purely

movement was, curiously enough, entirely unknown to the Elizabethans) trammelling themselves by a series of pedantic and artificial rules, the function of which was to reduce to a minimum the effects possible to poetic art.

But this change of form was accompanied by an equally extraordinary change of subject and of treatment. Here, again, where all had been liberty, where no bounds of space or time, no regulations of any kind, had curbed the erratic inclinations of the poets, they suddenly and wilfully shut themselves up between walls of rule, and abandoned the wild woods for stately and mechanical circuits around the box-walks of a labyrinth. For the direct appeal to Nature, and the naming of specific objects, they substituted generalities and secondhand allusions. They no longer mentioned the gilly-flower and the daffodil, but permitted themselves a general reference to Flora's vernal wreath. It was vulgar to say that the moon was rising, the gentlemanly expression was, "Cynthia is lifting her silver horn." Women became "nymphs" in this new phraseology, fruits became "the treasures of

---

exotic, and, even in the hands of Campion himself, neither natural nor successful. I would at the same time guard myself from being supposed to think, though for convenience sake I speak of iambics and dactyls, that we possess real metrical quantity in English.

Pomona," a horse became "the impatient courser[1]." The result of coining these conventional counters for groups of ideas was that the personal, the exact, was lost in literature. Apples were the treasures of Pomona, but so were cherries too, and if one wished to allude to peaches, they also were the treasures of Pomona.

This decline from particular to general language was regarded as a great gain in elegance. It was supposed that to use one of these genteel tokens which passed for coin of poetic language brought the speaker closer to the grace of Latinity. It was thought that the old direct manner of speaking was crude and futile; that a romantic poet who wished to allude to caterpillars could do so without any exercise of his ingenuity by simply introducing the word "caterpillars," whereas the classical poet had to prove that he was a scholar and a gentleman by inventing some circumlocution such as "the crawling scourge that smites the leafy plain."

[1] It may be noticed that it is in the *Cyder* of John Philips (written in 1699) that this pompous and allusive language is first used without stint or shame. Philips united two strains of influence, that of Waller and that of *Paradise Lost*, and introduced into Augustan poetry the sub-Miltonic phraseology which took so fast a hold of the eighteenth century. He had not learned, however, to avoid the exact expression, and names his peaches and walnuts like a market-gardener.

Shaftesbury introduced this exaggerated elegance of diction into the field of prose, and his success increased the foppishness of the poets. It made their vices inveterate, and in course of time the desire politely to avoid saying what was meant reached a height that was quite ridiculous. In the generation that succeeded Pope really clever writers spoke of a "gelid cistern" when they meant a cold bath, and "the loud hunter-crew" when they meant a pack of fox-hounds, and then at last the public began to crave a more direct form of utterance.

To detect and to ridicule,—sometimes most unfairly,—these peculiarities of the classical school, has, however, become a commonplace in the present generation. We know perfectly well, there is not a text-book that fails to instruct us, that the guarded generalities of eighteenth century poetry were bald and insipid. But we must be careful to discriminate. This indirectness, these strange, unnatural forms of circumlocution, were not in themselves characteristic of the classical school alone; all poetry, the most romantic poetry that ever was written, has hated to be forced to call a spade a spade. Shakespeare is quite as far removed at times from straightforward reference to his subject as Armstrong or Darwin, but the difference lies in the presence or absence of liberty of action.

Shakespeare says "sore labour's bath," but he likes also to say "sleep," simply, if he chooses; and he likes to feel free to say "balm of hurt minds" as well. The classical poet, on the other hand, must not only avoid the direct word, he must select one circumlocution and keep to it. His principle is restriction, ingenuity, a strait-laced elegance; the romantic poet's principle is liberty even though it lead to licence.

The secret of the enigma that a whole generation meekly and even eagerly consented to clip its own wings and subside into servitude, is primarily to be found in the word we have just used, licence. The people of the seventeenth century were weary of liberty, weary of the unmitigated rage of the dramatists, cloyed with the roses and the spices and the kisses of the lyrists, tired of being carried over the universe and up and down the avenues of history at the freak of every irresponsible rhymester. Literature had been set open to all the breezes of heaven by the blustering and glittering Elizabethans, and in the hands of their less gifted successors it was fast declining into a mere cave of the Winds. The last efflorescence of the spirit of humanism had taken that strange form which it found in the hands of Lyly, Marini, and Gongora, and the brief vogue of this wonderful heresy, with its extravagance, affectation, and preciosity, had but hastened on the certain and necessary reaction. When the leaders of literature began to write as Donne and Crashaw[1] did, it was absolutely inevitable that other leaders should soon begin to write like Waller and Dryden.

But there was more in the change to a classical taste than can be understood merely by a reference to our local schools of poetry in England. When Waller purified his verse of ornament and arranged it in distichs, he was unconsciously doing what was simultaneously being done in the other leading nations of Europe. It will perhaps help us to understand the change in England, if we glance briefly, in the first place, at some of her neighbours.

If a change was needed anywhere, it was in Italy, where the emptiness of the later Petrarchists, the insipidity of the pastoral poets, the monstrous

---

[1] One example will serve as well as a dozen, and the reader may amuse himself by turning to Crashaw, who writes a poem of thirty-one stanzas on the Weeping of the Magdalen, in which he calls her eyes "parents of silver-footed rills," "heavens of ever-falling stars," "Heaven's spangles," "nests of milky doves," "two walking baths," "portable and compendious oceans," "wells into which the Lamb dips his white foot," and "Time's hour-glasses;" while the tears themselves are "rivers of cream," "a brisk cherub's breakfast," "richest pearls," "thawing crystal," "sorrow's best jewels," "simpering sons of those fair eyes, your fertile mothers," and as many more unlikely things as the reader's curiosity can wish for.

extravagances of Marini, had reduced imaginative literature to the lowest ineptitude. But the soil of Italy was too thoroughly exhausted to produce a Dryden or a Pope, and the real reaction there was one against poetry altogether. A sort of classical revival, however, was attempted at the close of the sixteenth century by Chiabrera, who in disdaining the folly of the Marinists, and in trying to recall his countrymen to a Greek simplicity, attained a position somewhat analogous to that of Cowley. But he stood alone until Filicaja came, and Italy presents us with the spectacle of a literature too effete and nerveless to undergo the process of even a classical change. When at last the precise manner of that school was introduced, it was Parini, who, fresh from the study of Pope, attempted to graft an English bud on to the worn Italian stock. It is plain, therefore, that for the first time since English poetry had begun to exist, Italy had no help to give her in her literary revolution.

We turn to the Teutonic nations. In Germany, in Denmark, in Sweden, there could at least be no exhaustion of the soil, for here modern poetry had not begun to exist. Here we might expect a young literature, fresh in all the colours of the morning, to arise with healing in its wings. But, as though, on the eve of the horrors of the Thirty Years' War, Protestant Europe refused to be glad, nothing more cold or dull or decorous can be imagined than that First Silesian School with which modern German poetry begins. The very year before the great war broke out in Bohemia, Martin Opitz sounded the first note in his treatise *De Contemptu Linguae Teutonicae*, in which he entreated his countrymen to revert to the German tongue for poetry. He briskly supported his preaching by practice, and inflicted on the taste of his time reams of deadly couplets, strictly classical in taste, alexandrines with alternate male and female rhymes, all about nymphs and satyrs and the didactic Muse[1]. He took his cue directly from Holland and France, while Sweden and Denmark took their cue from him. The three first modern poets of the three countries, Opitz (1597—1639), Stjernhjelm (1598—1672), Arrebo (1587—1637), are as rigidly classical, didactic, and anti-romantic as it is possible to be, and they all belong to the

---

[1] The close of his flat and vapid romance, *Zlatna*, 1624, is almost pathetic in its aspiration:

> So würd ich meine Vers' auch wol nicht lassen liegen,
> Gar bald mit Mantua biss an die Wolken fliegen,
> Bald mit dem Pindarus; Nasonis Elegie,
> Doch zuvoraus genant als meine Poesie.

Here is a great flutter of singing-robes, but the hoof peeps out.

generation of Waller. So much we may note in passing.

Holland was the sole Teutonic country that already possessed a modern literature, a literature springing from the Renaissance. And here we seem nearer to England, for during the first half of the seventeenth century several literary courtesies passed, in a variety of ways, between Starter and Dekker, between Huyghens and Donne, between Vondel and Milton. The robust poetry of Holland underwent no sudden change or development, for two reasons. In the first place, humanism had originally and universally lost more of its bloom and grace in coming to Holland than in coming to any other country; secondly, the temper of the Dutch, except for one very brief and dubious moment at the end of the sixteenth century, was never romantic at all, but didactic or else farcical and melodramatic[1]. The Dutch had works answering more or less to those of Marlowe and of Ben Jonson, but nothing that recalls Spenser or Shakespeare. Their principal work therefore was, not to

---

[1] The Dutch have this year (March 16, 1885) celebrated the tercentenary of their greatest dramatist, Brederô. The English play which approaches nearest to the works of this man is Jonson's *Bartholomew Fair*; the humour of Brederô is the humour of Ostade, or of Terence read through the eyes of Ostade.

eliminate fantastic beauty, but to polish the execution of their verses, and this Vondel did slowly, through an interminable life of labour, all down the first three-quarters of the seventeenth century. At the close of his career, a classicism exactly answering to ours had invaded all Dutch literature, but it had come unobserved, and had been outstripped by the like tendency in England.

Something might be said of Spain, whose drama continued to affect our own. But we pass on to France, which is here mentioned last, because it has been customary to take for granted that the change in English poetry was entirely caused by the influence of France. I have quoted the other countries of Europe to show that there is no need to look for so strong an operation of the French mind in England, since every other country was, in one form or another, depressed, subdued, exhausted by rules and colourless ambitions at that very same time. England and France have occupied more attention than any other countries, but mainly because of their superior vitality, and the splendour of their production. It is, indeed, a strange thing that at the moment when England, under the cloud of her civil war, retired from the notice of Europe, she should be drawn into a species of literary alliance with the nations of the

Continent. But so it was, and in the singular unison of the aim which actuated Malherbe (1555—1628), Waller, and Opitz, we see the action of an intellectual force far deeper than the rage of leaguers or the ambition of a Gustavus Adolphus. And our reply to the question why this movement began first in France would be that at the final decline of the Renaissance it was France that stood at the intellectual head of Europe.

To admit this it is plainly necessary to admit that this change from the romantic to the classic was a step forwards, a necessary element in the progress of the human mind. The critic who should make this admission must be prepared to find himself in opposition to all the accepted canons of the last seventy years. He must be ready to be charged with paradox, the love of enunciating what is manifestly absurd, with applauding a change that gave us Cowley in exchange for Spenser. I hope that before this inquiry is concluded I may bring forward reasons for a view that at first sight appears so ridiculous. In the meantime we are occupied with France. I do not myself believe, or see any reason for suspecting, that the change to classicism in England was originally started by direct influence from France, any more than from Germany or from Holland or from Spain. It should be stated that the date of the beginning of that change must now be placed much earlier than it has hitherto been the custom to place it. In my next chapter, I shall show, by irrefragable proof, that Waller was writing didactic occasional poems in distichs which were often as good as Dryden's ever became, at least as early as 1623. Now Malherbe, with whom by universal consent the fashion for correct versifying and the exclusion of ornament set in, was not at this time a poet known even to the French public. A few of his pieces had come to light, but he had published no book: he was simply a fructifying centre of influence, just as Rossetti lately was in London for twenty years before he printed a book.

Malherbe's poems did not appear in Paris till 1630, two years after his death, and at least nine years after Waller, in his mother's country-house in Buckinghamshire, had discovered almost all that was to be learned about the fabrication of smooth and balanced couplets. Moreover, when Malherbe is spoken of as a polisher of the couplet, it leads us to suspect that his works have been more read about than read. It is, in fact, a very curious circumstance, which I do not recollect to have seen noted by any critic, that this great leader of the precise style in poetry, this harbinger of Boileau and

Racine, wrote less in alexandrines than any other French poet on record. Except one solitary fragment[1], of no importance, I do not think a single copy of verses in the conventional French distich has been attributed to Malherbe. Of the possible influence of St Amant on Waller, some ten years afterwards, something may presently be said, and there is no question at all that when the Revolution drove the Royalist English poets to Paris and Rouen, they eagerly studied their French contemporaries and predecessors; but then they had already formed their own style. I do not believe that Waller and Sidney Godolphin and Denham were in the very smallest degree affected by the French revolt against the poetry of the Renaissance when they opened their campaign against the romantic school at home. I am persuaded that it was the result of one of those atmospheric influences which disturb the tradition of literature simultaneously in all the countries of Europe alike, and that it was a much more blind and unconscious movement than that which towards the close of the eighteenth century impelled all the literatures of Europe to throw off the chains which they had adopted one hundred and fifty years before.

[1] The lines, addressed to Mme de Rambouillet, which were inserted in the letter from Malherbe, published in *Le Recueil de Lettres nouvelles* by Faret in 1627.

We return, then, to England, and to our date 1623, the year of the publication of the first folio Shakespeare, and of the composition of Waller's earliest couplets. An examination of the records of the Stationers' Company will help us nothing in forming a notion of the state of English poetry at that date. For some reason or other the publication of verse in the third decade of the seventeenth century was extremely slack, though preceded and followed by periods of great publishing activity. The new king, Charles I., was averse to the writing of poems; he would stroll up to young bards in the gardens of Oxford, and would say to them, "I saw thy copy of verses on her ladyship's eyebrow. They were good, vastly good! See to it that thou write no more." Such compliments were not encouraging to unfledged versemen, and whether from this or some other reason, the imprint 162— is rare on books of poetry, even of dramatic poetry. With one accord the poets of the Marini and Gongora school, who were then in the ascendant, desisted from publication till long after this. Phineas Fletcher, Carew, Herbert, Habington, and Suckling, all of whom claim to be leading writers of the second and third decades of the century, made no public appearance until the fourth, while Herrick waited until late in the fifth, as did Waller himself. From a purely bibliographical point of view, therefore, the title-pages of the poets are sadly misleading, and 1623 seems really to belong rather to the old generation of Shakespeare than to that of the so-called metaphysical school.

It was, in fact, a moment of exhaustion and transition in the book-trade. The day of the romance-writers and pamphlet-mongers was over; sixpenny plays and novels and verse-romances were no more sold over the counter. The gentlemen that had asked for "all Greene's works, ay! and all Nash's too" were dead, or old and gone away into the country. Even Shakespeare's *Venus and Adonis* and Lodge's *Rosalind* were beginning to lose their vogue. Books were more expensive, more cumbrous in form; education was spreading, the taste for knowledge was taking the place of that innocent curiosity and romantic simplicity which had made the fortune of the Elizabethan booksellers. Already the shadow of the great political crisis was beginning to darken the horizon, and men were troubled in their minds, seeking for exact information, interested in travels, in philosophy, above all, in theology. The great vogue of the Puritan divines was beginning, and almost the only verse which succeeded was put into the form of plays, cheaply printed, and hawked about in little dingy quartos, with a rough paper cover stitched round them, at the doors of the theatres.

There were interesting people enough to be met with, but there were no Boswells. Literary curiosity was a thing forgotten, although the preceding generation had to some degree possessed it. Sir Aston Cockaine, that egotistical poetaster, mentions that he knew all the men of that time, and could have written their lives had it been worth his while. The exasperating creature wrote bad epigrams and dreary tragi-comedies instead of doing this. In country places one or two of the generation that had seen Spenser and Shakespeare arise were still alive—Gabriel Harvey, Lodge, Barnfield, old men who were to give no further sign of life. The dramatists showed more vitality, though most of them held back their plays from publication until the thirties. Yet Webster's glorious *Dutchess of Malfy* belongs to our year 1623, and Jonson, Middleton, Chapman, and Heywood were still at work. Massinger was just emerging, and Ford was about to emerge. A whole troop or phalanx of tragic and comic playwrights was preparing to add its quota to the verse of the Donne and Marini school.

Meanwhile, though so little was published, a great deal was read. Each University, but Cambridge in particular, was a hotbed of poetry. The exciting, fantastical, hysterical canzonets of the great Dean of St Paul's were eagerly passed from hand to hand[1], and were as seed that sprung up in the breasts of dozens of ardent young writers. Poetry was no longer a profession, it was a cultus. A certain order of conceits was a shibboleth, which the public not only did not understand, but was not expected to understand[2]. Poetry began to be written for poets, for the elect, for a circle; and this was one of the deadly effects of that curious embargo upon publication of which I have spoken. Utter disregard was paid to unity, to proportion, to extent. In the great generation there had been too little regard for these qualities. Without profanity be it spoken, Sidney's *Arcadia* is dreadfully amorphous and invertebrate, and Macaulay's

---

[1] There was no edition of Donne's *Poems* printed earlier than 1633, but their impress on the poetry of the preceding generation is strongly marked.

[2] Henry More, in 1642, ushers in his Cambridge epic, the *Psychozoia*, with the usual defiance of the vulgar reader:—

    I strike my silver-sounded lyre,—
    First struck myself by some strong fire,—
    And all the while her warning ray
    (Reflect from fluid glass) doth play
    On the white banks. But all are deaf
    Unto my Muse, that is most lief [dear]
    To mine own self.

difficulty of being in at the death of the Blatant Beast would never have been propounded if the *Faery Queen* had not been so long that it is really excusable not to be aware that the Blatant Beast does not die. But if the *Arcadia* is shapeless, what are we to say of *Oceana?* and let not him call the *Faery Queen* tedious or dull who has never grappled with Phineas Fletcher's *Purple Island*. This masterpiece, with the charming mysterious name, is an allegory in twelve cantos, describing the body and functions of man :—

> "His lungs are like the bellows, that respire
> In every office, quickening every fire;
> His nose the chimney is, whereby are vented
> Such fumes as with the bellows are augmented."

So Quarles prattles away in a foolish poem of congratulation to Fletcher, but the author of the *Purple Island* himself strikes a much more lofty note, and for page upon pompous page describes, to a group of nymphs and shepherd-boys, who sit around him on a little hill of daisies, the tedious and inaccurate geography of this Isle of Man, with all its ridiculous and unseemly towns and lakes and rivers.

We know the poets of this early Caroline period almost entirely by extracts, and their ardour, quaintness, and sudden flashes of inspiration give them a singular advantage in this form. The sustained elevation which had characterized Shakespeare and Spenser, and even in some degree several of the chief of their contemporaries, had passed away, but still the poets were most brilliant, most delectable in their purple patches. That same much over-estimated Phineas Fletcher rises in his more natural and more felicitous moments to a rare echo of the luxurious Spenserian sweetness. This was strikingly the case with the lyrists. Carew, Lovelace, and half-a-dozen more are known to all lovers of poetry, not by their books, which are in the hands of but few persons, but by those matchless exceptions which criticism has lifted from their grotesque miscellanies, and has preserved in anthologies. It is quite right that they should live by those pieces, and I should be the last to wish to break one leaf away from their never-too-ample bays. But it seems to me mere pedantry, and pedantry of a particularly unwholesome kind, to pretend that the works of all the Marinist or so-called metaphysical poets of the reign of Charles I. are not excessively unequal in merit, and constantly ready to sink into unpardonable bathos or swell into equally unpardonable bombast. And this inequality goes so far, and pervades the literature of the period so completely, that even the verse-writers who have never taken any rank, in their own day or since, have their flashes of intense romantic beauty. I stretch my hand to my bookshelves, and I take down the first Caroline volume that I touch. It happens to be John Mason's tragedy of *Muleasses the Turk*, a mere bibliophile's curiosity. Nobody, so far as I know, from the date of its production to the present hour, has ever commended a word of it. I feel as though John Mason's ghost, after a silence of two hundred and fifty years, might be breathing hard by my side at the excitement of resuscitation. I glance along the pages and I read

> "Our life is but a sailing to our death
> Through the world's ocean; it makes no matter then
> Whether we put into the world's vast deep
> Shipped in a pinnace or an argosy."

That is very fine, surely! But is *Muleasses*, therefore, a good play? We look a little further and we find one of the personages, under the pressure of a certain annoyance, giving the following directions to his confidant:—

> "Thy fears keep in
> My trembling soul; it does not leave my breast.
> Mount to the flaming girdle of the world,

And fetch me lightning, I will swallow it!
Snatch from the Cyclops balls of Etnean fire
And I will eat them! Steal thunder from the clouds
And dart it at me! Quaff Stygian Nonocris,
And I will pledge thee."

It was this want of sobriety, of propriety, of common sense, which prepared the way for a prosaic reaction. The dramatists were primarily to blame for this, and especially the tragic dramatists; and early in the reign of Charles I. almost everybody essayed to be a tragic dramatist. The playwrights of the great generation had pitched their note high; no one can deny that Shakespeare himself is often only saved from the charge of extravagance by the rush of his intellect, by his unparalleled tact and persuasiveness of style, and by his fortunate genius. He says things which might be monstrous, if the human race did not immediately consent to break records, as athletic people say, and to begin experience again from Shakespeare's point of view. But if the greatest of the poets of the world ran a risk from the turbulent instincts of the age he lived in, the lesser men, the immeasurably lesser men, that followed him, had no chance of keeping their heels on solid ground.

In estimating this quality of sobriety, of common sense, in poetry, we are somewhat at a discount in this age, and a critic who holds it healthy to be calm and discreet in poetic writing may still find himself brought face to face with a fiery indignation. The reaction against the bondage of the eighteenth century still gives us a tender partiality towards what is exaggerated, violent, and bombastic. Still, even in this matter, I think our general taste is progressing in a salutary direction. Fifteen years ago it used to be all the fashion among young men of poetic aspirations to affect the tragedies of Cyril Tourneur. The name was an agreeable one, the plays were very rare and difficult to meet with, and accordingly Cyril Tourneur became a kind of watchword of the higher culture, like Botticelli. Now Cyril Tourneur has been reprinted, with admirable care, by a very distinguished scholar, and I notice that his name becomes rarer and rarer on the lips and pens of the enthusiastic.

Without expressing the least disrespect towards a writer in whom a variety of critics have found much to praise, I am bound to say that the existence of Cyril Tourneur appears to me to be one little reason more, by the way, why the classical reaction should be regarded as absolutely inevitable. Cyril Tourneur is a regular raw-head and bloody-bones, a vampire of literature, a purveyor of yells and dead-men's bodies and churchyard curses. The passages which attracted the admiration of Charles Lamb are sudden felicities, such as I have just said can be discovered, though, I allow, in fewer numbers and in less sustained brilliance, in a vast number of examples. But the general tenour of his writings is so monstrous, so confused, so obscure, that there are whole pages which might have been written by a Dyak of Borneo who had strayed into the school of Lycophron.

I would desire to recommend to anyone who holds that English poetry at the beginning of the seventeenth century was in a quiet, healthy condition, and needed merely to be allowed to go on its course, a *chef-d'œuvre* of Cyril Tourneur's called *The Transformed Metamorphosis*. I remember the shouts of joy among the elect when this masterpiece was first discovered in a unique copy some twelve years ago. Well, the editor and fondest admirer of Cyril Tourneur admits that the excessive obscurity of *The Transformed Metamorphosis* " arises as much from the abnormal and grotesque mould in which the whole poem is cast as from the hideous jargon in which it is written[1]." These are the words of a leading admirer of the school of James and Charles, and I seize them as a text for my parable. I am asked why the literature of the seventeenth century shut itself up in bondage, why it subjected itself to stiff and artificial rules, why it confined itself to dry and obvious themes; my answer is, because of the abnormal and grotesque mould in which all but the best passages of poetry had come to be cast, and because of the hideous jargon in which verse was written[2].

---

[1] Here is a stanza :
"From out the lake a bridge ascends thereto,
  Whereon in female shape a serpent stands,
Who eyes her eye, or views her blue-veined brow,
  With sense-bereaving gloses she enchants,
And when she sees a worldling blind that haunts
The pleasure that doth seem there to be found,
  She soothes with leucrocutanized sound."
Leucrocutanized is good ; but what does it all mean ?

[2] The early critics of the Restoration saw this very clearly, and it made them blind to the beauties of their predecessors. Knightly Chetwood (1682) remarks that what English poetry has need of is

"one who license can restrain,
Make civil laws o'er barbarous usage reign,
One worthy in Apollo's chair to sit,
And hold the scales, and give the stamp of wit,
In whom ripe judgment and young fancy meet
And force the poets' rage to be discreet,
Who grows not nauseous while he strives to please,
But marks the shelves in our poetic seas."

But it was not merely the want of proportion and sustained style, it was not merely the intemperance and unwholesomeness of the poets, which called for drastic reform, it was also their want of sympathy with the ruling tastes of the people. The growth of an instinct for liberty, the rapid increase of political curiosity, which marked the decade before the Civil War, and which Charles, by his unimaginative obstinacy, fostered as studiously as if he had been a paid agent of revolt, this widening of the intellectual conscience gave Englishmen quite a new interest in what was actual and vital to themselves. In the great generation of Elizabeth there had been diffused over the people something of the temper and curiosity of a very brilliant child. In the search for romantic excitement Verona had been as interesting to them as London, or more interesting. The novels that pleased best were those in which the scenes revealed some forest of palm-trees dividing the Empire of Russia from the Kingdom of Peru, some wild strand where the waves cast pearls and ambergris on the stormy sea-board of Bohemia. Probability, what we call actuality, went for nothing; like children, the Elizabethans demanded an illusion, but were quite indifferent as to the sober basis of that illusion. Perhaps the only sign which their imaginative literature gave of any germ of realism, in the modern sense, was afforded by the domestic tragedies, on crimes of passing interest, which were now and then played, with startling crudities of effect, in the smaller theatres.

But in the next generation a complete change came over the national mind. In the great period, a friend of Shakespeare, Michael Drayton, had written a serene and lovely poem, in his leisurely way, on a period of English history. If I mention *The Barons' Wars* here, it is not with any notion of comparing it with the crude epics of the next generation, with the *Purple Island* and the *Levite's Revenge*, but merely to show how totally distinct the notion which so elegant and accomplished a poet as Drayton had of the function of history was from what appealed to the conscience of the men who fought against ship-money. To do so, I will quote one stanza out of *The Barons' Wars*, a stanza taken almost at random, a brick out of that stately building. The Earl of March is dying and he writes a letter to the Queen :—

"Most mighty Empress, sdaign not to peruse
 The swan-like dirges of a dying man,
Unlike those raptures of the fluent Muse
 In that sweet season when our joys began,

> That did my youth with glorious fire infuse,
>   When for thy glove at tilt I proudly ran;
> Whereas my startling courser strongly set
> Made fire to fly from Hartford's burgonet."

This is the first of seven stanzas, all in the same style, of which the letter is composed. We are given ten more, in which the agitation of the Queen on receiving it is described. It is all charming poetry, full of lovely and chivalrous images, and a passionate music runs through it. But the reader observes that it is not history, that it would be equally interesting as a letter of any dying soldier to any lady he had loved, and that it is obviously written to please readers who took a great deal more interest in hearing about a handsome earl who died for love of a fair queen, than in the effect that earl's insurrection may have had in improving the condition of the House of Commons, or than in the political results of that Queen's partiality for her fatherland. In point of fact, Drayton's poem would have been almost as charming and almost as popular if Mortimer had been named Amandus and the Queen Amanda.

To comprehend the mental condition which made the classical reaction possible, we must endeavour to realize this complete alteration in the temper of the readers of poetry. And one great feature of this change we have not yet indicated. With this desire for more exact knowledge, with this widening of the political sympathies, with this craving for more simplicity and more regularity in literature, there came in another sentiment which was not so interesting or pretty. This was the decline of the spirit of adventure. The poetry of the Elizabethans had been very largely animated by this spirit. It had been written by men of adventure, by soldiers such as Sidney, by buccaneers such as Lodge and Raleigh. Now all that was over; the poets would go no more a-roving, and if they were to be soldiers in the future, it was in a grievous and unromantic fight with their own flesh and blood, in fields that their fathers had tilled in friendship side by side. The brief period of splendid lawlessness on the high seas in the days of Elizabeth had told on the literature of this country, as the adventures of the Greeks told on the tragedies of Æschylus, or as the deeds of Icelanders who went a-viking told on their drapas and their sagas. But to this brief period of intoxication, a time of depression and collapse was bound to follow.

Without, then, too ingeniously building up what should be, from a knowledge of what was, we can on the whole put ourselves pretty distinctly into the place of a young man who, about 1623, should find himself moved to head a reaction against the ruling taste of the day in verse. In much of what has been already said, of course the view of the supposititious young man, rather than my own view, has been dwelt upon. We can imagine such a young fellow, in some Cambridge College, returning from the company of a circle of friends who had been passing MS. poems of Dean Donne from hand to hand in an ecstasy,—we can imagine him saying to himself, " Are they mad to praise this coarse and obscure *Progress of the Soul?* Are we doomed for ever to have to endure such verse as this,—

'Virtue is soul, always in all deeds, all ?'

Is this craze for calling heaven and earth to witness the ingenuity of a conceit to spread like a canker through every member of our literature?" He would question thus, and we must not blame him if, in his anger, and in his craving after style, after proportion, he should neglect those eminent beauties which we can perceive readily enough, and which have made us of late too tender to the faults of the early portion of the seventeenth century.

If it were my duty here to call attention to what is good in those interesting writers of the age of Charles, the task would be an easy and a gratifying one. But I desire to keep close to the question which is before us, the causes which led to the classical reaction. I cannot blind myself to the fact that one of the principal of these causes was what I have indicated, the inequality and alembicated character of the poetry in vogue. The young man I have imagined would turn to his *Ars Poetica*, and would smile to think that the very monsters which Horace painted by the light of prophecy were come to the birth at last. The lovely woman ending in a fish, what simile could better describe the beautiful moral monstrosity of Fletcher's *Faithful Shepherdess?* Where does the dolphin gallop through the woods and the wild boar breast the waves, if not in the cantos of the *Purple Island?* Who so ingenious as Herbert or Carew in painting the cypress when it was a shipwreck they were commissioned to paint? All the commonplaces of that wonderful prelude of Horace would come back to the young man as singularly, as pitifully, characteristic of his own age, and he would have little inclination to praise the technical beauty in the purple patch itself, be it cypress or dolphin or woman. He would rather be inclined to dream of a straightforward prosaic poetry, closely bound down by the unities, by the rules of composition such as Aristotle and Horace have given them; and would reply to the ancient question, Is it Nature, is it Art, that leads to a praiseworthy poem? by asking another question, "What do my contemporaries answer?" And when they had all vociferated "Nature," he would draw his toga around him, with as Roman an air as he could affect, and would quietly decide for "Art."

The young man to whom I have been alluding has not been a mere figure of rhetoric; he existed, and his name was Edmund Waller. To him and to his peculiar qualities of mind and character happens to be due the first initiation into that great change, that turning topsy-turvy of all poetic literature, which was henceforth to be the main intellectual labour of the seventeenth century. Waller was not a great, or attractive, or inspiring man, although of course he must have had exceptional powers and singular opportunities to have effected what he did effect. But he is the hero of this whole volume. My readers will be forced, if they pay me the compliment of listening to me, to hear a very great deal about him, and to become tolerably intimate with his talents and his character. I need not here, at the close of a chapter, say anything more about him, but the last minutes which we spend together now may be devoted to the speculation, Why was it not John Milton, instead of Edmund Waller, to whom it was given to revolutionize poetry in England?

Here, again, as everywhere where we look closely into the historic development of literature, we see the value of dates, and the paramount importance of a clear chronological sequence. Broadly speaking, it was because Milton was born three years later than Waller, and did not so rapidly come to maturity, that we did not receive from him a classical bias which would have been something very different from Waller's. The time was ripe, and when, in 1623, these first experiments in distich were made, the public taste was like touchwood, and caught the fire to let it steadily smoulder. In 1623 Milton was a schoolboy still; six years passed before the *Nativity Ode* was written, and there he displayed himself simply as the most brilliant of the Marinists.

At Horton, in his famous five years' retirement, he afterwards withdrew from this erroneous school of conceits, and wrote the lovely polished poems which we know. But he was out of the world, while the leaders of the new school were in it, and they with their facile prosaic manner gave the public something much more popular, though far less noble, than Milton's withdrawn and solemn organ-music. The side which the more eminent poet took in politics separated him still more from those who, in the far greater majority, were the supporters of literature, and when he began, in his own words, at the summons of God's secretary, Conscience, to "embark in a troubled sea of noises and hoarse disputes," he was himself taken away from the sphere of poetical composition for eighteen laborious years. So that Milton's noble figure will accompany us all down the course of our inquiry, but at a distance, neither approving nor disapproving,—the restless and irritable temper of the age through which he lived being, as little as that of the age into which he was born, sympathetic to his peculiar serenity of mind, the mind that would not condescend to little things.

WALLER AND SACHARISSA.

WALLER AND SACHARISSA.

IN that treasury of obsolete opinion and indispensable data, the *Biographia Britannica*, as published in the year 1766, we find the following startling sentence:—"Edmund Waller, the most celebrated Lyric Poet that England ever produced." If we remark that this confident judgment was expressed in so authoritative a quarter more than a century and a half after the birth of the poet for whom such supremacy was claimed, and that the readers of this phrase were divided from Waller as far as we ourselves are from such old-fashioned poets as Akenside and Falconer, we may well be disposed to marvel at the duration of a fame that has been thoroughly eclipsed at last. Nay more, we may surely feel a curiosity to discover what it was about this half-forgotten poet which can have impressed the public for more than a hundred years with a sense of his magnitude and importance. And, indeed, the inquiry which we are now engaged in making into the phenomena which attended the great change from romantic to classical poetry in England can only be carried out by giving due and careful attention to the career and character of a lyric poet who reigned supreme until the classical taste declined, and who has been discarded ever since the romantic taste revived.

In our last chapter we saw what elements were collected to form the body of English poetry in the decline of such phases of the Renaissance as had reached our shores. In the general disorganization and solution of the old forms of romantic poetry, there was needed an astringent which should brace the textures and condense the solids of literature. In the great romance of Rabelais, we find Ponocrates purging Gargantua with the hellebore of Anticyra to make him forget all that his other masters had taught him[1]. This harsh restorative, this herbal secret of forgetfulness, was presented to English poetry in the nick of time by what we must be allowed to call, for want of a

---

[1] "Lequel le purgea canonicquement auec elebore de Anticyre, et, par ce medicament, luy nettoya toute l'alteration et peruerse habitude de cerveau."—*Gargantua* i. 23.

better term, the genius of Waller. While the function of most leaders of literature is to refresh and extend the mind, to explore new fields of beauty, to throw the windows of the soul wide open to fresh airs from the world of nature, it was Waller's duty to capture and imprison the imagination, to seize English poetry by the wings, and to shut it up in a cage for a hundred and fifty years, to win a position as the leader of imaginative literature by narrowing its scope and rigidly reducing its resources.

Of late years, ever since the beginning of the present century, indeed, it has been customary to disregard entirely the position claimed and won by this remarkable man. It may easily be conceded that his is not a sympathetic figure; but the time has surely passed when we can reject writers from their stations in the evolution of literature because their writings or their characters are unalluring to ourselves. Here is a man of whom, after the lapse of a century and a half, it still seemed a commonplace to say that he was the most celebrated lyric poet that England ever produced; we may reject him as we will, we cannot allow ourselves to deny that his historic position is of the very highest interest. We must examine his career with attention, that we may discover what there was about the man himself which could subjugate his own contemporaries with so strong a spell, and his writings, that we may find out what it was in them that appealed to generation after generation as something more elegant and captivating than the poetry of Shakespeare, of Spenser, and of Milton[1].

Edmund Waller was singularly fortunate in his birth and extraction. In the reign of James I., among so many upstart dukes and earls, he possessed the dignity of a wealthy country gentleman ennobled by a long line of honourable landed ancestors. The family tree of the Wallers was a flourishing and stately vegetable at least as far back as the reign of Henry VI. A very distant progenitor, a Mr Richard Waller of Spendhurst, had enjoyed the charge of that noble prisoner, Charles of Orleans, after the battle of Agincourt, and some vestige of the influence of the indefatigable and indolent maker of rondeaux may have descended from father to son. At that time, and long afterwards, the family estates were in Kent, but towards the close of the reign of Elizabeth we find them situated in the heart of

---

[1] "Inter poetas sui temporis facile princeps," says the inscription at Beaconsfield, though Herrick, Milton and Dryden were "sui temporis."

Buckinghamshire. Mr Robert Waller lived at Amersham, or, as it was then spelt, Agmondesham, a borough, even then decayed, seated upon Milton's little classic river Missbourn.

When he wished to marry, Mr Waller went a few miles westward to the village of Hampden, near Princes Risborough, where Mr John Hampden, of that ilk, enjoyed a position very similar to his own, and where he received the hand of his daughter. Mr Hampden possessed a young son, who then, and for a long time afterwards, was conspicuous only for his "jolly conversation" and for his warm pursuit of field-sports, but who is now known to all the world as the famous patriot John Hampden. By the means of this marriage, it will be observed, the Wallers became connected with the family of Cromwell, and thus even before his birth those social complications began which were so to vex the trimming spirit of the poet.

As the nephew of John Hampden and the cousin of Oliver Cromwell, then, Edmund Waller was born into the world on the 3rd of March, 1605, at a country-house belonging to his father, and called Coleshill, which was then in a fragment of Herts, but is now absorbed again into Buckinghamshire. As he grew up at this house, the child was within an easy walking distance of all the little boroughs which were to be identified with him in mature life: Amersham, which he was to represent in parliament; Wycombe, where he was to live and dispense hospitality; Beaconsfield, where he was to die and to be buried. A pastoral and woodland country, watered by little rivers flowing southward to the Thames, and hallowed to us all by more sentimental association with the greater names of Milton and Gray, yet not so characteristic of the writings of those high-flying spirits as of the graceful, precise, and mundane poetry of Waller.

The poet's father made thrifty use of the large fortune which descended to him, and when he died, which was during Edmund Waller's infancy, he left his only son an income of £3,500 a year, a property which was nursed by his careful mother all through his childhood and youth. The consequence was, that when Waller came of age he was in possession of one of the most splendid private fortunes in the country, nor until the end of his long life did all his crosses and vicissitudes prevent the money from gathering under his feet wherever his fate pursued him. There never was a child so plainly born with the traditional silver-spoon in his mouth as Waller, and since the world began there have been very few poets indeed that have been half so rich as he. His mother, whose Christian name is lost, sent him to Eton at an early age, and transferred him thence, probably about 1618, to Cambridge; he was entered a scholar at King's College, where there is now no record of his entrance. Tradition informed the author of his Life that he was extraordinarily proficient in all his studies while at the University, which he left early that he might take part at once in public life.

We are, however, met here by a serious difficulty. The accepted story is that Waller entered parliament, as member for Amersham, at the age of sixteen,—that is to say, in 1621. According to this legend, the young poet was one of those summoned on the 16th of January in that year to consult with James I. on the crisis in Bohemia and the general distracted state of Christendom. There is no primâ facie absurdity in this, for babes and sucklings found their way into the House of Commons in those days, and no questions asked. But the poet's tomb in Beaconsfield Churchyard, the inscription on which was carefully compiled by Rymer the historiographer from documents placed in his hands by the family, states that Waller entered parliament, as member for

Amersham, when he was not yet eighteen[1]. This would point to the beginning of 1623, by which time, as we shall presently see, he was already deeply interested in affairs. But unhappily for these stories, cold fact steps in and mentions that Amersham had ceased to return members in the reign of Edward II., and that its burgesses did not resume the right of election until 1624, when Hakeville and Crewe represented it at Westminster during James's fourth and last parliament. There are two ways out of the difficulty: the one that Waller attended the third parliament *sub silentio*, which his prudent mother might think a wise mode of securing a political education; the other, that he was duly returned, but for some other borough than Amersham.

But whatever were the youth's exact relations to the court and the houses of parliament, we know that they were of such a nature as could only be attained by a personage who united precocious talents to unusual social advantages. On the 30th of December, 1621, before he had completed his seventeenth year, Waller was witness to a

---

[1] The phrase of Rymer is precise, "*Nondum octodecenalis* inter ardua regni tractantes sedem habuit, a burgo de Agmondesham missus." This inscription was made in 1700, at the expense of Mary, the poet's second wife, and Edmund his son.

strange scene which imprinted itself deeply upon his memory, and which he vividly described long afterwards to Dr Birch. It was the day upon which James I. had gone to Whitehall, and had practically dissolved his third parliament by tearing the protestation of the Commons out of the journals of the House. He said that he hoped he might hear no more about liberty of speech.

At dinner-time Edmund Waller, coming into court, found the King seated at table, with the Bishops of Winchester and Durham standing behind his chair. Still out of temper with the obstinacy of the Commons, the King growled out to the two prelates, " My Lords, cannot I take my subjects' money when I want it, without all this formality in Parliament?" Neale, Bishop of Durham, hastened to reply, " God forbid, sire, but you should; you are the breath of our nostrils." Whereupon King James turned and said to the venerable and stately Lancelot Andrewes, " Well, my Lord of Winchester, what say you?" "Sire," was the answer, "I have no skill to judge of parliamentary cases." The King persisted, " No put-off, my Lord; answer me presently." " Then, Sire, I think it is lawful for you to take my brother Neale's money, for he offers it." Waller tells us that the company was pleased with this politic reply, but the King was in no temper for wit. He brooded over it, and some time afterwards he allowed himself, with that coarseness which was native to him, to crack a vulgar jest at the expense of Bishop Andrewes' smartness.

This anecdote and a single copy of verses are all that are left to us of this earliest period of Waller's career. The copy of verses is so poor and tiresome that I should despair of interesting my readers in it, if it were not understood that in the course of our present inquiry we are not mainly on the outlook for what is beautiful or witty in itself. These verses, which Waller published as his earliest and which may be attributed to the year 1621, have a structural peculiarity which is of the most curious importance. In his Epistle to the Earl of Orrery, prefixed in 1664 to the anonymous edition of the *Rival Ladies*, Dryden drew attention for the first time, but in language which our later knowledge can scarcely improve, to the main peculiarity of Waller's poetical style. "Rime," he said, "has all the advantages of prose, besides its own. But the excellence and dignity of it were never fully known till Mr Waller taught it: he first made writing easily an art; first showed us how to conclude the sense, most commonly in distichs, which, in the verse of those before him, runs on for so many lines together, that the reader is out of breath to overtake it."

Dryden here notes the fact to which I called attention in my last chapter, and which I am afraid I must insist upon at the risk of being tedious—the principle of the structure of the romantic poetry was overflow, that of the classical poetry was distich. It is therefore of extraordinary interest to find Edmund Waller, as early as 1621— that is to say, nearly a quarter of a century before anyone else in England did so—writing his copy of verses "To the King on his Navy," in distichs as correct and monotonous as any that he composed to the day of his death; in thirty-two lines we find but one overflow [1].

[1] "Where e'er thy Navy spreads her canvas wings
　Homage to thee, and peace to all she brings;
　The French and Spaniard, when thy flags appear,
　Forget their hatred and consent to fear.
　So Jove from Ida did both hosts survey,
　And when he pleas'd to thunder part the fray;
　Ships heretofore in seas like fishes sped,
　The mightiest still upon the smallest fed," etc.

Written in 1621, these lines might have been signed in 1721 by some versifier of the school of Addison. But I confess that I cannot persuade myself to receive them as an untouched product of the reign of James I. The line about the French and Spaniard points to Charles I. and to 1634. There is nothing difficult of acceptation in the idea that Waller revised an old poem to suit a new occasion.

The next poem of Waller's to which we can supply a date, and in this case the application is certain, forms even a more curious and valuable text for criticism. I believe that the main reason of Waller's popularity and influence was the prosaic, the anti-imaginative, function which he conceived for poetry. It appeared to him that verse, and verse of a more precise kind than had hitherto been written in England, was a proper vehicle for the celebration of facts, public or private, of passing interest. This no one before his time had perceived, except a few Jacobean scribblers, devoid of art, like Taylor the Water poet, whose influence had been *nil*. It was distinctly an inspiration for a lad of eighteen, in the winter of 1623, when Ben Jonson and Chapman and Drayton were the poets most in vogue, resolutely to sit down without a model to write a long poem on the exciting incident of the moment, the danger Prince Charles had just escaped on his return voyage from Spain.

The occurrence is well remembered: Charles was rowing back by night from Santander to his own vessel, the "Prince," when the wind suddenly rose and very nearly swept the barge out to sea. Sir Sackville Trevor, on board the "Defiance," fortunately became aware of what was happening, and threw out ropes with lanterns attached to them, one of which was caught by a rower on Charles's barge, and the "heroick Prince," as Waller calls him, was saved. It is very interesting to compare the poem with the published account of the incident; we see that the verses possessed, and were intended to possess, the lively actuality of a newsletter. The whole political situation is lightly touched, phase by phase; the Prince's gallant object in Spain, the diplomacy of Olivares, the dubious and coy position of the Infanta, the attitude of France, all are discussed in language which may seem florid to us, but which had the charm of novelty and reality to the gentlemen and ladies of James's court, among whom the verses were circulated in manuscript. I must be allowed to quote a few lines, as a specimen of the style of this interesting and vivacious poem. It is supposed that, during the peaceful moments that preceded the storm, while Charles was still riding through the streets of Santander amid the noise of bells and cannon, the sea-god Arion occupied himself in soliloquizing as follows regarding the ancestors of the god-like Prince:—

"While to his harp divine Arion sings
    The loves and conquests of our Albion kings,
    Of the fourth Edward was his noble song,
    Fierce, goodly, valiant, beautiful and young,

He rent the crown from vanquished Henry's head,
Raised the white rose and trampled on the red,
Till Love, triumphing o'er the Victor's pride,
Brought Mars and Venus to the conquered side."

The prosody of such lines as these is quite undistinguishable from that of the classic school from 1660 to the close of the seventeenth century. Dryden proceeded no further than this in the mere execution of the distich, and it was only in the hands of Pope that it received a further polish and rapidity. We find Waller here not merely turning off his serried couplets with complete ease and indifference, but surpassing in his earliest efforts what was done all through their lives by his more immediate pupils. Such writing as this, which Waller was master of in 1623, was not imitated by a single poet for nearly twenty years; yet he persisted in it, and lived to see the entire English Parnassus absorbed by it. We must admit that the man who could effect such a revolution, and show from youth to age so intrepid a consistency of manner, deserves the closest attention from the student of style.

It was consistent also with his isolated habit of mind that Waller does not seem to have consorted with any of the poets of his own youth. A rhetorical address to Ben Jonson goes far to prove that he was not acquainted with the only writer who is mentioned in the poems of his youth and middle life. It has been assumed, on slender evidence, that Sir John Suckling translated into Latin one of the Sacharissa poems, the version being printed by Waller as his own. Less proof of Waller's association with his poetical peers could hardly be adduced, and Suckling was, after all, a golden swashbuckler of the gardens of Whitehall more than a person of letters. The truth seems to be that Waller held himself resolutely aloof from the contemporary literature of the age, and cultivated those dry distichs of his by some curious unsympathetic inspiration, the exact nature of which we shall never know.

His thoughts during these boyish days seem to have been politically ambitious. His great wealth drew him naturally to court, and in August, 1625, he sat in the House of Commons for another of the local Buckinghamshire boroughs, for Chipping Wycombe. Parliament met its new King on this first occasion at Oxford, and the boyish Waller, not yet of age, was a sharer, no doubt, in the panic regarding the plague and the grumbling about the noisome lodgings which occupied the short course of a session that must have seemed to him like a summer holiday. He little realized, we may be sure, that he was witnessing the first throes of that mighty struggle in which the constitution of England was presently to be rent into shreds. Next February he represented Wycombe at Westminster, in Charles's second parliament, and the following year Amersham in the third.

In 1627 he came before the public in a very strange way. Ann, the daughter and sole heiress of a wealthy citizen of London of the name of Banks, appears to have attracted general attention by the combined charms of her appearance and her fortune. The Court itself took this interesting young person under its patronage, and deigned to discover a husband for an heiress so distinguished. This candidate for Miss Banks's hand was a courtier of the name of Crofts, whose suit was considered to be gained, when Waller, then aged two-and-twenty, coolly stepped in, and married the fair lady in the teeth of Whitehall. The Earl of Clarendon tells us that this incident caused Mr Waller to be famous to a degree which he had not attained by his wit, nor his fine parts, nor his poetry.

It is probable that it also caused him to be looked upon at Court with some degree of ill-will, for we learn that in 1628 he retired with his young wife into Buckinghamshire, to his house at Beaconsfield, and gave himself up to study. In the winter of that year he wrote another of his gazetteer poems, the piece *On his Majesty's receiving the news of the Duke of Buckingham's death.* In the choice of his subject Waller once more showed a tact which served him well with his own immediate public, but which has lost its charm for posterity. Buckingham, it will be remembered, had just breakfasted at Portsmouth, when Felton met him in the passage and stabbed him to the heart. Charles I. was only five miles off, at Southwick, and when Sir John Hippesley brought the news, he was still at morning prayer. The story current at the time, which Clarendon repeats and Waller versifies, is that the King, when the news was whispered to him, remained kneeling without change of countenance until the function was over.

"The sacred Wrestler till a blessing given
 Quits not his hold, but halting conquers Heaven,"

says Waller, and deftly compliments the monarch at once upon his presence of mind and his tenderness.

"Such huge extremes inhabit thy great mind,
 God-like unmoved and yet like Woman kind."

Contarini, as quoted by Mr Gardiner, says that Charles did in fact show panic on his countenance, but it seems certain that he did not stir till prayers were ended, when he rushed to his bedroom, flung himself on the bed, and gave way to a torrent of lamentations.

Waller's retirement into the country was identified with his sudden friendship for a remarkable man, George Morley, long afterwards Bishop of Worcester and then of Winchester. Waller had lately been admitted into that society of learned and wealthy persons which was known as Lord Falkland's club. At one of the meetings of this body a noise was heard in the street, and looking out of window the members saw a young man being arrested by bailiffs. They were told it was "a son of Ben Jonson," this being the name given to themselves by a group of young University wits who affected to be the poetical offspring of the author of *Volpone*. The debtor was brought in to the club, and proved to be a relation of Waller's own, George Morley, a penniless student of Christchurch, Oxford, as learned, witty, and needy as a man could be. Waller was charmed with his acquaintance, and the end of the meeting was that the poet persuaded the student to come down to Beaconsfield and share his retirement. This Morley did, and for ten years spent his life in the enjoyment of hospitality alternately with the

Wallers and with the Earl and Countess of Carnarvon. He lived to be a very old man, and under the Restoration rose in the Church to those episcopal dignities by which he is best known. But in these early days he was secular and humanistic in his proclivities, and it is said, and this is strongly confirmed by Lord Clarendon, that it was mainly due to him that Waller seriously undertook to cultivate poetry. It is certain that the ten years he spent with Waller were those in which the great bulk of that writer's verses were composed, and it may further be noticed, as a link in the chain of events, that Morley was the first cousin of Sir John Denham, who was to be Waller's earliest pupil in poetry.

Waller, on retiring from public life, left his mother in the family mansion in the town of Beaconsfield, and built for himself another, a quarter of a mile away, at Hallbarn. Here his wife died at the birth of their first child, and left him a widower at twenty-four. Morley was now his constant and chief companion, and with him he drowned grief and ambition for a year or two in a profound study of the writers of antiquity. He was first drawn out of his retirement by his public passion, if I may be allowed to use such a term, for the lady he addressed as Sacharissa, and whom he believed that he had made as famous as Petrarch made his Laura[1].

Sacharissa was an after-thought for Dorothea, the name under which Waller originally celebrated the charms of Lady Dorothy Sidney, the eldest daughter of the Earl of Leicester. She was the grand-niece of that romantic Sir Philip Sidney who wrote the *Arcadia* and who died at Zutphen nearly thirty years before her birth, though when the latter event took place, Waller's commentator Fenton was unable to discover from the register at Penshurst. We may be sure that it was not much earlier than 1615, and that when Waller began to address her about 1632, she was still quite young[2].

The course of this true love, though so stately and imposing, was not much troubled, it would appear, by mundane temper. There is no trace of emotion, of doubt, of terror on the lover's part.

---

[1] Exactly a hundred years later, we find Sacharissa still named among the immortal ladies of poetic history. Elijah Fenton, in 1730, confidently sings:—

"Secure beneath the wing of withering time,
Her beauties flourish in ambrosial prime;
Still kindling rapture, see! she moves in state;
Gods, nymphs and heroes on her triumph wait."

[2] The card now (July 1885) attached to the beautiful portrait of her, by Vandyke, at Penshurst, says that she was born in 1617; but this seems to be conjectural. In this picture she appears as a lovely and buxom young shepherdess of about twenty.

The lady is cruel, the bard is despairing, and after the pompous suit has been carried on without incident of any kind for seven years, we find the lady suddenly falling in love with a real flesh-and-blood young gentleman, of only nineteen summers, whom she promptly marries. It must be confessed that, as we shall presently see, nothing in the process of this suit became Waller so well as the manner in which he made his bow on abandoning it. In the meantime we must give ourselves to the examination of this, the most famous cycle of love-poems which the seventeenth century possesses.

The moralists who ever and again remind us that the really great is the materially small, and that Athens and Weimar ruled the world of letters, may point if they will to the Sacharissa Poems as an example of the truth of their position. It is quite extraordinary to find when we sift these famous pieces from the body of Waller's writings, how slender a bundle they form. The immortality of the fair, the cruel, the disdainful Sacharissa hangs upon no more than ten direct poetical addresses, and about half as many indirect testimonies to her beauty and her scorn. The long heroic poem, called *The Battle of the Summer Islands*, it is true, is dragged behind the car of the cruelty of Sacharissa by means of a few allusions that look sadly as though they were manufactured to satisfy a public demand, but of genuine lyrics dedicated to Lady Dorothy Sidney we do not possess enough to form the thinnest of pamphlets. It is, of course, possible that as none of these poems were printed until long after the suit was over, and as Waller affected indifference for merely literary glory, many were written which the young lady and her friends neglected to preserve. It seems to me probable, however, that Waller did not address her very often, or upon any occasions except those on which he was sure to make a direct social sensation.

There is nothing tender, nothing personal in any of these famous verses. They form a straightforward and manly statement of devotion, after its kind, but they are as far from passion as from indiscretion. The lover addresses his mistress as if in the hearing of a large and courtly throng of persons, who seem lightly to applaud a suit so elegant and so genteel. He is as deliberate, as allusive, as calm and as gentlemanlike as Magdelon in the *Précieuses Ridicules* wishes her suitor to be, and we have an indescribable sensation that the verses are composed and recited by a person whose wig and gloves and shoe-strings are invariably in the most admirable order. We feel in reading these Sacharissa poems that we are slipping into the classical atmosphere, with its horror of the personal note. Not thus have the English poets hitherto made love, Drayton with his

"Since there's no help, come, let us kiss and part,"
or Donne with his

"O more than Moon,
Draw not thy seas to drown me in thy sphere."

There is no whisper here, no trouble of the pulses, no mystery. We are positively astonished to hear this grave and wealthy young man at Beaconsfield discoursing so placidly and decorously of his sorrows:—

In vain, he says:—

"In vain I struggled with the yoke
Of mighty Love; that conqu'ring look,
When next beheld, like lightning strook
My blasted soul; and made me bow
Lower than those I pity'd now.
 So the tall stag, upon the brink
Of some smooth stream about to drink,
Surveying there his armèd head,
With shame remembers that he fled
The scornèd dogs; resolves to try
The combat next: but if their cry
Invades again his trembling ear,
He straight resumes his wonted care;

> Leaves the untasted spring behind,
> And, winged with fear, outflies the wind."

We feel that nothing could be more gracefully turned; we seem to hear a murmur run through the audience of "Charming! Charming!" but the last thing that crosses our mind is to sympathize with the stricken deer.

To see in how conscious and how public a spirit the whole suit was conducted, we have only to examine the very curious piece entitled *The Story of Phœbus and Daphne applied*. Here Waller calls himself Thirsis:

> "Thirsis, a youth of the inspirèd Train,
> Fair Sacharissa loved, but loved in vain;
> Like Phœbus sung the no less amorous boy,
> Like Daphne she as lovely and as coy."

The confident conceit of these verses is very remarkable. He positively ventures to say that he, Mr Edmund Waller, is pursuing the flying Nymph "with numbers such as Phœbus' self might use" and with an eye turned directly to the auditorium, does not even hesitate to declare that

> "What he sung in his immortal strain,
> Though unsuccessful, was not sung in vain."

Many of the poets of the seventeenth century, from Shakespeare downwards, prophesied for the objects of their passion an immortality in their verse, but this of Waller's is a singular instance of a poet promising himself immortality, in spite of the object of his verse. This resolute self-aggrandizement, too nobly born to seem vulgar or fatuous, must be taken into consideration as a factor in Waller's poetical success[1]. From the summit of a position to which his wealth, his social graces, his wit and his adroitness had raised him, he gravely announced himself to the world as *Phœbi Sacerdos*, not a priest only, but the high-priest of Apollo.

We can form but a very vague idea of Lady Dorothy Sidney from the Sacharissa poems; she is everywhere overshadowed by Waller himself. We are told that she can sleep when she pleases, and this inspires a copy of verses; but later on we are told that she can do anything but sleep when she pleases, and this leads to another copy of verses which leave us exactly where we were when we started. We are told of a misreport of her being painted, of the likelihood of her being painted, in another sense, by Vandyke, of a crowd in which she nearly became crushed, of how her

---

[1] Malherbe, his French prototype, had possessed the same sacerdotal dignity. In his sonnet to the King he had remarked:—
    Les ouvrages communs vivent quelques années,
    Ce que Malherbe écrit dure éternellement.

lover keeps away from her lest he should love her more. There is nothing positive, nothing concrete; we move about among rumours that are unfounded and events that never happen. Yet it is noticeable that each arquebusade of wit, each cunning attack upon this battlemented beauty, is made at a moment when the eyes of society are upon her and him. A great poet of the generation before Waller's had said—in lines which have no appearance of having been intended for publication, and which in fact were never published during his lifetime—

"'Twere profanation of our joys
To tell the laity our love."

The Sacharissa cycle is at the extreme opposite of this tender and intimate manner of poetry. If the laity is not listening, and if the laity is not largely composed of persons of quality, Waller is silent as a lover.

And yet the Sacharissa poems contain some exquisite numbers, and it is to be noted that, under the influence of George Morley, Waller lost for a time that persistence in the heroic distich which had distinguished his early youth, and was to be the unbroken habit of his middle and later life. The *Song to a Rose* is well known, but deserves repetition :—

"SONG.

    Go, lovely rose!
Tell her that wastes her time, and me,
    That now she knows,
When I resemble her to thee,
How sweet, and fair, she seems to be.

    Tell her that's young,
And shuns to have her graces spy'd[1],
    That had'st thou sprung
In deserts, where no men abide,
Thou must have uncommended dy'd.

    Small is the worth
Of beauty from the light retir'd:
    Bid her come forth,
Suffer herself to be desir'd,
And not blush so to be admir'd.

    Then die! that she
The common fate of all things rare
    May read in thee:
How small a part of time they share,
That are so wondrous sweet, and fair!"

---

[1] The syllables "graces spy'd" drag painfully on the tongue, and I remember to have heard the greatest living authority on melodious numbers suggest that Waller must have written "graces eyed." The first edition of 1645, however, has, by an obvious misprint, "grace spy'd," and I believe that what Waller wrote was "grace espy'd."

Less known, but almost as perfect, is "On a Girdle."

"ON A GIRDLE.

That which her slender waist confin'd,
Shall now my joyful temples bind;
No monarch but would give his crown
His arms might do what this has done

It was[1] my heaven's extremest sphere,
The pale which held that lovely deer:
My joy, my grief, my hope, my love,
Did all within this circle move!

A narrow compass! and yet there
Dwelt all that's good, and all that's fair:
Give me but what this riband bound,
Take all the rest the sun goes round[2]."

The power of writing songs like these survived the introduction of classical taste in England, as it had done in France. Gradually it declined, until for a short time during the preeminence of Pope, it may almost be said to have disappeared; but throughout the remainder of the seventeenth century the gift of song-writing was present among

---

[1] "Is," in the edition of 1645, where the present tense is kept up through the poem.

[2] In 1645:—
"Give me but what this riband tied,
Take all the sun goes round beside."

the English poets. It is in the non-lyrical departments of poetic art, especially in didactic, descriptive, and dramatic verse, that we have to look for the change that now was imminent.

The next example of Waller's work which comes before us, the heroic poem called *The Battle of the Summer Islands*, throws more light upon the development of this change than the love-songs to Sacharissa. It is therefore more interesting to us, although a comparatively insignificant work in itself. It is the most considerable poem, in length, which Waller ever published, and deals, in three cantos, with a sort of pseudo-Homeric subject, a battle between the islanders of Bermuda and two spermaceti whales that had got stranded in a shallow bay. It used to be taken for granted that Waller visited Bermuda about this time, or in 1640; it is almost certain that he was one of the Adventurers, or landlords, into whose plantations the archipelago was divided. But Major-General Lefroy, who has lately chronicled the early history of the islands in two copious volumes, has found no trace of the poet's visit, and disbelieves in it. He points out that Waller makes blunders in his description, such as no real observer could make; he takes the low cedars which covered the islands to be cedars of Lebanon, and talks of "the lofty cedar which to Heaven aspires:" while he promises to lull the savages with Sacharissa's name although there was not a single savage there to lull. It seems, however, to have escaped Major-General Lefroy that the report that Waller visited Bermuda cannot have been set afloat by the fact that he wrote the *Battle of the Summer Islands*, from the simple circumstance that he represents himself in that poem not as having yet seen Bermuda, but as longing and hoping to do so[1].

My own belief is, that the astute Waller, having property on the islands, and having, as I should conjecture, embarked money in the company which was started in 1637, under the auspices of Governor Chaddock, wrote his heroic poem, and circulated it among wealthy and noble friends, as an advertisement. Until that time, passion, ambition, the urging sense of harmony or beauty, had inspired English heroic poems; but this was in future to be

---

[1] His words are:—

"O how I long my careless limbs to lay
Under the Plantan's shade, and all the day
With amorous airs my fancy entertain,
Invoke the Muses, and improve my vein!"

My conviction is that he no more reached Bermuda than George Herbert or Bishop Berkeley did. These islands have attracted much notice from English men of letters, but have proved difficult of access. Tom Moore reached them, but quitted them soon and eagerly.

by no means *de rigueur*. Half a century later, when the classical transformation was almost complete, Hobbes in his essay *Concerning the Vertues of an Heroique Poem* laid down as the first rule for its composition that it should possess "perspicuity and facility of construction." The heroic poems of the Elizabethan and Jacobean ages,—*The Barons' Wars* of Drayton, the *Albion's England* of Warner, the *Ovid's Banquet of Sense* of Chapman, for instance,—had possessed various brilliant and touching qualities, irregular force and sudden brilliance of style, but certainly not what Hobbes means by "perspicuity and facility of construction." The *Arcadia* of Sidney is not facile, the *Christ's Victory and Triumph* of Giles Fletcher is not, in this sense, perspicuous, but Waller's *Battle of the Summer Islands* is, just as *The Hind and the Panther* of Dryden is perspicuous, and *The Dunciad* admirable for its facility of construction.

Waller's little epic is a perfectly straightforward narration in three parts, the first containing a highly-pitched description, the exaggerated fulsomeness of which irritates the historian of the Bermudas, of the commercial and natural advantages of that colony; the second containing an account of the stranding of the whales; and the third of the battle itself. Nothing could be pitched more definitely in the key of common-sense. We are told with scrupulous fidelity,—the puff of the oranges and grapes and melons being finished,—what exactly happened on this curious occasion:—

> "The Boat which on the first assault did go,
> Struck with a harping Iron. the younger foe;
> Who, when he felt his side so rudely gored,
> Loud as the Sea that nourished him, he roared;
> As a broad bream, to please some curious taste,
> While yet alive in boiling water cast,
> Vext with unwonted heats, boils, flings about
> The scorching brass, and hurls the liquor out;
> So, with the barbèd javelin stung, he raves,
> And scourges with his tail the suffering waves."

It is very difficult in reading these lines to realise that when they were written Dryden was an infant, and that the men were still in the prime of life who had known Shakespeare and had served him in the production of his romantic plays.

In 1639, the year after the composition of *The Battle of the Summer Islands*, Lady Dorothy Sidney suddenly grew tired of hearing Waller

> "twang his tiresome instrument
> Above her unconcern,"

and she married Henry, Lord Spencer, who was presently created Earl of Sunderland. However young Sacharissa may have been when Waller first addressed her, she must have been by this time a good deal older than her bridegroom, who was only nineteen. After four short years of married life, her young husband was killed fighting for his King at the battle of Newbury, and Sacharissa settled down for forty years as a widow, devoting herself to the education of three children, and never losing sight of her old persistent poet-lover. There is a story extant to the effect that when they were both very old the Dowager Duchess of Sunderland rallied her friend by saying, "Ah! Mr Waller, when will you make such beautiful verses about me again?" "Madam," said the poet, with more of gallantry, we must hope, in his eyes than in his words, "when your ladyship is as young again!" But before we turn from the Sacharissa episode which has taken so prominent a part in the legend of Waller's life, we must quote the letter which he wrote to Lady Lucy Sidney, the younger sister, in July, 1639, when Sacharissa had just been married.

"MADAM,

"In this common joy at Penshurst I know none to whom complaints may come less unseasonable than to your Ladyship; the loss of a bed-fellow being almost equal to that of a mistress: and therefore you ought, at least, to pardon, if you consent not to, the imprecations of the deserted; which just heaven no doubt will hear!

"May my Lady Dorothy, (if we may yet call her so,) suffer so much, and have the like passion for this young Lord, whom she has preferr'd to the rest of mankind, as others have had for her! And may this love, before the year go about, make her taste of the first curse impos'd on womankind, the pains of becoming a mother! May her first-born be none of her own sex! nor so like her, but that he may resemble her Lord as much as herself!

"May she that always affected silence, and retiredness, have the house fill'd with the noise, and number, of her children; and hereafter of her grandchildren! and then, may she arrive at that great curse so much declin'd by fair Ladies, old age! May she live to be very old, and yet seem young; be told so by her glass, and have no aches to inform her of the truth! And when she shall appear to be mortal, may her Lord not mourn for her, but go hand in hand with her to that place, where we are told there is neither marrying, nor giving in marriage; that being there divorced, we may all have an equal interest in her again! My revenge being immortal, I wish all this may also befall their posterity to the world's end, and afterwards!

"To you, Madam, I wish all good things; and that this loss may in good time be happily supply'd with a more constant bed-fellow of the other sex.

"Madam, I humbly kiss your hands, and beg pardon for this trouble, from

"Your Ladyship's most humble servant,

EDM. WALLER."

Among the poems which belong to the Sacharissa period, but show much more than the lyrics the classical tendency of Waller's taste, that *Upon His Majesty's repairing of Paul's* demands especial notice, because of its popularity, and the influence which it exercised upon younger minds. That Waller's poems circulated in MS. so widely as to enjoy positive popularity is proved by an allusion to this piece, which forms the earliest mention of Waller which I have been able to discover, and which preceded by three years the publication of the lines referred to. In the first anonymous edition of his *Cooper's Hill*, an edition in which the poet displayed the courage of his anonymity, Sir John Denham delivers himself of the following notable piece of criticism. He is standing on Cooper's Hill, and surveying the horizon, till he reaches the point where the cathedral cuts it:—

"Paul's, the late theme of such a Muse whose flight
Has bravely reached and soared above thy height;
Now shalt thou stand, though sword, or time, or fire
Or zeal more fierce than they, thy fall conspire,
Secure while thee the best of Poets sings,
Preserved from ruin by the best of Kings."

And for fear that his readers should not know who "the best of Poets" was, Denham adds a note, "Master Waller," a note in subsequent editions reduced to M. W. But here, in 1642, before Waller had printed a line, we find him boldly addressed as "the best of Poets" by the pupil who was treading most closely in his footsteps, and who, though ten years his junior, had outstripped him in the date of publication.

We must reserve consideration of Denham, however, until our next chapter, and glance for a few moments at the poem which called forth such eulogy from him. We find it to be of the class which we are beginning to expect from Waller— that is, an adroit and graphic account in graceful distichs of an event which was happening at that moment to entertain the public. The commissioners had met to discuss the question of rebuilding St Paul's in 1632, and in the following spring the mean buildings which were clustered around the cathedral, and which clung to its sides like parasites, were bought and destroyed. The poet plays about the subject with elegance unusual even in him, who seldom wrote otherwise than as a courtier and a gentleman. He refers to the wonders of old, the cities built to music, the magic instrumentation of Orpheus and Amphion.

"Those antique minstrels sure were Charles-like kings,
Cities their lutes, and subjects' hearts their strings,
On which with so divine a hand they strook
Consent of motion from their breath they took."

The augury is perhaps a little unhappy, to us who can see this Orpheus-like Charles presently torn to pieces by the outraged liberties of England, and that comely head floating down the Hebrus of the Revolution, but the allusion—for a classical allusion—was pretty, and the verse wonderfully polished. With singular skill Waller interweaves this strain of panegyric, this warm cloud of incense waved under the nostrils of Charles, with accurate and prosaic information about the edifice described. He tells us that the Choir is nearly finished,— which conveniently helps us to the date, 1635; that the western end, with its stately Corinthian portico, was raised at the King's personal expense, and what share private bounty had in paying for the rest of the architecture.

We have but to consider how difficult it would

have been for one of the romantic poets, his predecessors, to have proceeded with a theme like this, to feel the importance of the change in favour of grace, common-sense, and precision[1]. The Muse of the romantic period was like the fleet and lovely Atalanta, who is conquered by the apples flung on either side of her path; she catches sight of these tempting accidents of style, these shining images, allusions, and conceits, and she falters in her flight, pauses, and is left behind by her heavier and duller companion. The charm that Waller had for his contemporaries seems to me to have been the charm that a sensible, calm person of elegant tastes and manners may possess for one who has been for some time thrown exclusively into the society of over-excited, hysterical people, who have wearied him with their demands upon his enthusiasm and his sensibility. The seventeenth century was labouring under a plethora of ebullient genius; it craved a little rest, a period of common-sense and literary decorum.

The remainder of Waller's career before his exile at the Revolution belongs to politics and not

[1] It was very seldom that they would allow themselves to be entrapped into the treatment of public recent events, but observe the agonies and contortions of Carew in attempting to obey Aurelian Townsend, who had bidden him describe the death of the King of Sweden.

to literature, but we may close our present examination of his services by a brief survey of these years, in order that we may escape the need to return to them in our next chapter. For a little while Waller took a position in public affairs more prominent than that which any other English poet has attained, a position which might easily have placed him where Lamartine was placed long afterwards in France. When the breach widened between the Houses and the King, Waller found himself suspended between the two parties in a perilous isolation. There was a great deal to attract him in each party. Clarendon tells us that he was always welcome at court, because of his parts and courtesy, and because he had the tact never to ask for any honours or preferments. On the other hand, he was the nephew of Hampden, the cousin of Cromwell, a country gentleman who suffered as his neighbours did from the intolerable tax of ship-moneys. His subsequent fiasco made him contemned by each party, but a careful study of what Lord Clarendon, no quite unimpeachable witness, has written, and above all of Waller's own speeches in the House of Commons, leads me to believe that he was not a hypocrite or a traitor, in the worst sense, but a vacillating and trimming creature, dowered, like all poets, with a mixture of farsightedness and nearsightedness which was fatal to him as a politician. He saw that the statesmen of Charles had, in his own words, "dipped their dart in such a poison that, so far as in them lay, the commonwealth might never receive a cure[1];" he could not believe in the power of the nation to find an antidote, and, while believing the Houses to be in the right, he yet plotted to betray them to the King, because he thought their opposition was hopeless, and would merely launch England upon massacre.

In 1641, he wavered so far on the popular side, that he was chosen by the Commons to impeach Judge Crawley, on whom the sin of ship-money had been fastened. His speech was scathing in its eloquent denunciation of the venal lawyer, but it is almost the only proof we have of his adherence to Pym and Hampden. It was during the famous debate of February 8th, 1642, on the ecclesiastical petitions, that Waller seems to have made up his mind to quit the party which was presently to become that of Root and Branch. In company with Falkland and Digby, he took his place in the Episcopalian group which that debate created. Two months later his pungent questionings brought down on him a rough reply from Maynard, who

[1] "Speech in the Painted Chamber," delivered July 6, 1641.

roundly told him he had no business to sit in that house. In November he was still more publicly reprimanded for his outspoken criticism, and forced to apologise.

All that year Waller was noiselessly drifting closer and closer to the King. In 1642, he sent Charles £1,000 to Nottingham, to support his army, and throughout that year, according to Clarendon, "he spoke every day with impunity against the sense and proceedings of the House" of Commons. Yet the Roundheads seem to have trusted him no less than the Royalists, and after the battle of Edgehill, he was sent down with other free commissioners, to propose terms of peace to the King at Oxford. They found Charles walking in the garden of Christchurch, and all his companions being peers, Waller was the last to kiss the King's hand. Charles I. said, in a very marked manner, " Though you are the last, Mr Waller, you are not the worst, nor the least in our favour." There can be no doubt that these too-gracious words were but the prelude to one of those fatal confidences by which Charles lightly threw away the lives of his best servants, as a chess-player abandons his pawns. It is not to be doubted that before Waller left Oxford he was pledged to treason against the Houses of Parliament.

Lord Clarendon's account of the plot is confused and scanty[1], but we are enabled to follow the course of events with tolerable accuracy. Waller seems to have promised to use his influence to collect the Neuters into a body strong enough to paralyze the extreme party, and deliver the city into the King's hands. He made a proselyte of a gentleman named Tompkins, who had married his sister, and Alexander Hampden, a royalist, although of the popular family, actively espoused the same cause. The Earl of Portland was doubtless with them[2], and Lord Conway too; whether the great Earl of Northumberland actually pledged himself is matter of doubt. Tompkins, under Waller's direction, made a kind of census of the city trained bands, and counted up malcontents that could be trusted in every parish and ward. Finally, as far as we can gather through the mist of conflicting evidence, Lady Daubigny had been sent forth from Oxford, two months earlier, with a

---

[1] There can be little doubt that his relations with Portland induced Clarendon to be purposely vague in dealing with this portion of his subject.

[2] Prof. S. R. Gardiner has discovered an unprinted letter from Waller to Portland which seems to prove, beyond all doubt, that the latter lied when he asseverated his ignorance of the plot. He was one of those with whom Waller had been seen only too rashly whispering.

special pass, and carrying innocently in her bosom a commission from the King to various persons in London giving them command over the civic forces of London.

There were various accounts of the way in which the plot was discovered. One was that Waller's sister,—not Mrs Tompkins, but a Mrs Price,—was led to relieve her conscience by revealing the whole story to her chaplain, a strong presbyterian. Another was, that a man-servant of Tompkins', like a Puritan Polonius, hid behind the arras until he had heard enough to compromise the leaders. But the genuine one now appears from the D'Ewes MSS. to be that Lord Dover from Oxford wrote a rash letter to his wife, warning her to leave London, and that, a day or two later, a certain Hassel boasted that London would very shortly be in flames. At any rate, the mode of the disclosure of the plot was startling and almost theatrical. The parliamentarians were collected at morning-prayers on a solemn fast-day, May the 31st, in the church of St Margaret's, Westminster. A message was brought in from the Speaker, summoning all members to a special session of the House; there was much whispering and agitation, and most of those addressed left the church. D'Ewes, indeed, thought lightly of it, and would not go. But rumours of the most exaggerated description spread at once through London; Waller and Tompkins were arrested before nightfall, and a sketch of their plot was published by the House of Commons to allay popular alarm[1].

Waller's conduct under this sudden calamity was deplorable. He lost all presence of mind, all decency, all manliness. He confessed everything, and finding that all the others denied complicity, he overwhelmed the whole circle of his acquaintance in universal denunciation. He seems to have hoped to escape punishment by including half of England in his fault. He who had been so gallant, such a champion of beauty, in his mortal terror was poltroon enough to accuse a number of great ladies and to charge them with inciting him to this rebellion. His fright, to be sure, was only too well grounded. The Parliament was in no temper to be trifled with. A short way was made with poor Tompkins. He had a handsome house in Holborn; a gallows was promptly raised in the street in front of it, and there Tompkins was hanged. A like fate befell others far less deeply implicated than Waller, and the luxurious poet felt a terrible

---

[1] This pamphlet, which it would be interesting to possess, appears to have totally disappeared. Even Prof. Gardiner has never come across it.

sensation, no doubt, in the region of his neck. He was within a hair's breadth of being hanged, as it was; but his amazing cleverness and duplicity dragged him through. He professed to be so overwhelmed with remorse, that his judges allowed his case to be postponed till his frantic paroxysms of grief should have subsided.

When at last he did appear, July 4th, he claimed his right to be heard in the House of Commons[1]. He appeared in Westminster in a

---

[1] I am able to print, for the first time, an account of this extraordinary scene from an eye-witness. In the MS. Diary of Sir Symeon D'Ewes, under the date "July 4, Tuesday 1643," I find this account of Waller's appearance at the bar of the House:—

"He was all clothed in mourning as if he had been going to execution itself, his demeanour was also composed to a despairing dejectedness, and when he came to the Bar he kneeled down, and so continued kneeling, until myself and some others who stood near to the Bar bade him stand up. For his great fear that he should be executed for this conspiracy (which he much more deserved than Mr Tompkins his brother-in-law, who had already suffered, although he had been merely drawn into the same by the said Mr Waller whose sister he had married) did almost compel him to say or do anything, and certainly he would have deserved and would have found much more pity than he did, had he not a little before his coming to the House basely accused Algernon Earl of Northumberland to have been privy to this conspiracy, whom upon his first examination he had cleared, and yet divers of the House seeing his sad and dejected condition at the Bar whom they had formerly heard speak in public with so much applause, could not forbear shedding of tears. One thing was most remarkable, costume of the deepest mourning, in an attitude of utter despair; he seemed about to sink into the earth, and in accents of the profoundest humility he delivered a speech to the eloquence of which, as Clarendon has aptly said, he owed the keeping of his head as much as Catiline owed the loss of his to that of Cicero. He urged on the parliament the unwisdom of allowing the soldiers to try any member of that great House, "however unworthy and monstrous," and endeavoured to persuade them to take him under their own jurisdiction and to spare him. The accounts of this speech are not

that he did look exceeding well, the reason of which was easily guessed at by those who had heard of his secret actions, for, having been a widower many years, he was so extremely addicted and given to the use of strange women as it did for the most part alter his very countenance, and make him look as if his face had been parboiled, being naturally of a very pleasing and well-tempered complexion." D'Ewes goes on to say that six or seven years before Waller had been attacked by a fever, of which he was like to die, and that his aunt, Lady Scudamore, took the opportunity to speak to him very gravely about his profligate habits, whereupon Waller, with tears and great show of penitence, said that if his life were spared, he would turn over a new leaf. However, on getting well, he returned at once to his old ways, and on Lady Scudamore's expostulating with him, he told her, with great jocularity, that she ought to have known better than to trust to sick men's vows. Whereupon she warned him that calamity would fall upon him, and when the plot was discovered, she did not fail to visit him in prison and to point the moral. Waller's character does not improve as we turn upon it more and more the bull's eye of history. The reference to D'Ewes' words is *Harl. MSS.* 165, *fol.* 144.

creditable to human nature; the miserable Waller, crawling and fawning for his life, is a loathsome subject of contemplation, and we cannot wonder at the indignation of May, the tragic poet, who was secretary to the House of Commons at that time, and who has no contempt bitter enough for the way in which Waller, in his decent black, whined before his colleagues, "bewailing his offence, and thanking God that so mischievous and bloody a conspiracy was discovered before it could take effect."

The House, however, proved implacable. Waller was expelled from Parliament and handed over to the army to be court-martialed. He was condemned to death, but after long pleading and parleying, Essex consented to pardon him, with a fine of £10,000. He was ordered to leave the country instantly; he did not wait to be twice asked to go, but fled to France, and settled with his family at Rouen, early in 1644. With this we may take leave of him for the present; his exile was the close of the first act in the development of classical poetry in England.

THE EXILES.

THE EXILES.

THE earliest critics of our classical poetry never wavered in their allegiance to Waller and to Denham as the Castor and Pollux, the divine twin brethren, who first refined the art of verse and taught us Englishmen the graces. In dedicating his tragedy of *The Rival Ladies* to Lord Orrery, himself a rhyming tragedian, Dryden says: "The excellence and dignity of rime were never fully known till Mr Waller taught it; but this sweetness of his lyric poesy was afterwards followed in the epic by Sir John Denham, in his *Cooper's Hill*, a poem which, your lordship knows, for the majesty of the style, is, and ever will be, the exact standard of good writing." With the sweetness of Waller we are already acquainted. We must now introduce ourselves to this majesty of Denham, who demands our consideration all the more because it happened that a book of his was the first poetry published by the English classicists[1]. Waller's *Poems* were widely circulated from hand

[1] Appendix I.

to hand, but they remained in MS. until 1645. Denham's *Sophy* was published in 1642, and his *Cooper's Hill* later in the same year.

John Denham was ten years younger than Edmund Waller, towards whom in spite of all his literary successes he remained till the end of his life in the position of a pupil. His father, also John Denham, and a knight, was an English lawyer, who became Chief Baron of the Exchequer in Ireland, and who married the daughter of an Irish peer, Lord Mellisfont. The poet was born at Dublin in 1615 into a flourishing and luxurious condition, and he remained through his whole life a man of high social position and recognized quality. When the poet was two years old, his father was recalled to England, as one of the Barons of the home Exchequer, and Denham's early education was acquired in London. At the age of sixteen he was entered a gentleman-commoner in Trinity College, Oxford, and remained there until 1634. Anthony à Wood has preserved this quaint picture of Denham as an undergraduate: "He was looked upon as a slow, dreaming young man, and more addicted to gaming than study; they could never imagine that he could ever enrich the world with the issue of his brain, as he afterwards did."

There are no youthful verses of Denham's existing, nor any record that he wrote at Oxford. His first cousin, George Morley, the son of his father's sister, was living all this time in retirement with Waller at Beaconsfield, and we cannot doubt that it was through this relative that he became interested in the new school of poetry. The lyrics to Sacharissa were being handed about, and possibly Denham saw these; but it is Waller's exercises in the heroic couplet which have left a trace on his own work, and to which he actually refers with praise. In 1634 the young Denham was entered at Lincoln's Inn, it being proposed that he should follow his father's profession, the law. It would seem that he worked pretty closely under the paternal eye, and even apparently lived during these years, when he was not in London, in his father's house at Egham on the Thames, close to the gentle acclivity of that Cooper's Hill which he was to make so famous. Young Denham was bitten with the rage for gambling which infected so many clever youths in the seventeenth century, and references to which swell the jeremiads of the satirists. He was constantly stripped of all his allowance, and on his father's chiding him, and threatening to cut him off with a shilling unless he amended, he wrote a little *Essay against Gaming*, in which he eloquently declared that the very notion of gambling filled him with detestation. This was the more ingenious of him, because he was all the time as mad after cards as ever; his father, however, seems to have been pacified.

In 1636, at the age of twenty-one, Denham wrote the earliest copy of his verses which has been preserved. It is called *The Destruction of Troy*, and it is a paraphrase of the second book of the *Æneid*. He kept this piece in MS. for twenty years, and then published it, at last, with an elegant and pleasing essay on the art of translating[1], which is much more mature than the poem itself, and is probably of a much later date. The *Destruction of Troy* is one of those poems which baffle criticism. There is really nothing to say about it, and even if it were an excellent piece of writing, it would lie outside the range of our present inquiry, for it is written in the old, slipshod verse, against which Waller had already rebelled[2]. The preface, about the mode

[1] Appendix II.
[2] Even here, in occasional passages, the new prosody asserts itself. The last lines, however, I feel convinced, were added in 1656 :—

"Thus fell the King, who yet surviv'd the State,
With such a signal and peculiar fate;
Under so vast a ruin not a grave,
Nor in such flames a funeral fire to have;

of translating, is much more valuable, and if a collection be ever made of the first breathings of poetical criticism in England, this should certainly be included in it. The main point which Denham brings forward is the importance of securing the spirit, grace, and movement of the original writer, even at the risk of losing some of his exact expressions.

In January, 1638, the elder Denham died, and was buried at Egham. The poet, thanks to that smart little *Essay against Gaming*, inherited a fortune, and spent the next two or three years in squandering several thousand pounds. It is much to be regretted that we possess no record of these years, for we lack the link that should bind the author of the limping paraphrase of Virgil with the stately buskined writer of *The Sophy* and of *Cooper's Hill*. It is quite plain that he had by this time become acquainted, probably through the good offices of his cousin Morley, with the MS. poems of Waller. The *Sophy*, however, which was published in 1642, is not in the style of any particular work of Waller's. It is a tragedy in

> He, whom such titles swelled, such power made proud,
> To whom the sceptres of all Asia bowed,
> On the cold earth lies th' unregarded King,
> A headless carcase and a nameless thing."

This is in the mature style of Denham.

five acts, in blank verse, and although it is far from interesting or invigorating, we must conquer our repugnance, and allow our attention to rest upon it.

The *Sophy* is a very curious experiment, an attempt to enchain English drama as French drama is enchained, to relinquish all those privileges, those capacities for licence, which had made English tragedy the beautiful and bewildering thing we know. When it was published, the great dramatic school was just closing. Ford and Massinger were resigning the art which they had received from Webster and Fletcher into the hands of Shirley. There is no means of discovering now where Denham got the idea of the style of his play[1]. It is very brief and brisk; delayed by no

---

[1] The plot is borrowed from Sir W. Herbert's *Travels*. The same story was dramatised shortly after by Robert Baron, in his *Mirza*, published, without a date, apparently in 1647. Baron thus refers to Denham:—

"I am not ignorant that there is a Tragedy abroad of this subject, intitled *The Sophy;* but it may be said of me as Terence makes his Prologue to his *Eunuchus* speak of him (though in a cause somewhat different)

'sed eas fabulas factas prius
Latinas scisse sese, id vero pernegat.'

I had finished three complete acts of this tragedy before I saw that, nor was I then discouraged from proceeding, seeing the most ingenious Author of that has made his seem quite another story from this."

Mirza, which has never enjoyed the attention its cleverness

poetical passages, or lyricism, at all; it contains but one or two soliloquies, and those carefully prepared for effect, like Racine's afterwards. The language is stilted, but never vociferous; it runs on a level, with none of the usual English ups and downs. Variety of action is subordinated to the illustration of character exactly in the French style.

The question is, however, where can Denham have seen any French tragedies? He had not at that date left his own country, and French books, especially plays and poems, were very slow to cross the Channel. It would be preposterous to suppose him affected by Montchrestien, Hardy, or Rotrou; while the great Corneille, to whose tragedies *The Sophy* does bear a distinct affinity, was so exactly Denham's contemporary, that it is very difficult to admit the notion of his influence. Until the production of the *Cid*, Corneille had published nothing that Denham could possibly copy; is it or is it not within the range of credibility that between 1636 and 1642 Denham could have seen the *Cid?* There is, however, practically no resemblance between the two plays, and if Denham imitated Corneille at all, it must have

demands, is full of good poetical passages in the old blood-and-thunder style, and is noticeable, moreover, for what appears to me to be very early imitation of Milton's lyrics.

been in *Cinna*. I do not, however, believe that, curious as is the analogy, there was any actual prompting from France, but that *The Sophy* remains a solitary[1] specimen of the Seneca tragedy amongst the English drama of the age, just as the curious play of *Tyr et Sidon*, as Mr Saintsbury was the first to point out, remains a solitary experiment in romantic tragedy in seventeenth-century French.

We are told that on the publication of *The Sophy*, Waller said that Denham had "broken out, like the Irish rebellion, threescore thousand strong, when no one was aware, or the least suspected it." It is interesting to see Waller, who seems never to have praised his romantic contemporaries, instantly perceiving that this was a spiritual comrade of his own. We have already observed with how much tact Waller seized the passing events of the hour as topics for his poetry. Denham did the same, even in this tragedy about the Turk. He wrote it in the great year of suspense, 1641, and it is full of little allusions to current politics. It is certain— I shall presently be able to prove it—that Denham, though a staunch Cavalier, leaned towards the

---

[1] Half a century had passed since Daniel had written his choral tragicomedies, the *Cleopatra* and the *Philotas*, imitations, I suppose, rather of Jodelle's French than of Seneca's Latin.

party of peace. When he puts into the mouth of his Turkish lord these sentiments,

"It is the fate of princes, that no knowledge
  Comes pure to them, but passing through the eyes
  And ears of other men it takes a tincture
  From every channel; and still bears a relish
  Of flattery or private ends;"

it is impossible not to see him shaking his head over Charles's mad answer in July to the demand of the Houses for the removal of evil counsellors; and still plainer is the irony about the King, who has been so long divided from his subjects that he becomes a tale to them, and who, when he asks whether he is still beloved, is told that

"Still some old men
Tell stories of you in the chimney-corner."

Events hurried on, and, amidst the momentous bustle of the first years of civil war, it may surprise us to hear the little voice of poetry raised above the din. It was in 1642, the year before Chalgrove Field and Newbury, the year too before Waller's terrible and almost fatal collapse, that Denham published his celebrated poem of *Cooper's Hill*, a piece conceived in a mood as calm and philosophical as if the halcyons had been brooding over the placid ocean of English politics. This poem was so decisive a victory for the adherents of the classical school that we may call it their Marston Moor, and not too fantastically conceive Denham and Waller, for Waller certainly had a share in its execution, as routing the forces of the romanticists with their ranks of serried couplets. In spite of all successive attempts in the same style,—and they have been myriad,—*Cooper's Hill* still remains the most celebrated, though perhaps the last read of topographical poems.

It is not quite true, as all the Augustan critics used to aver, that no topographical poetry had been written in England before Denham. Drayton's *Polyolbion* and Browne's *Britannia's Pastorals* belong, no doubt, to altogether a different order; but it is very extraordinary if Denham had never read the *Penshurst* of Ben Jonson. There was, however, something to be distinguished between the praise of a great peer's house and the tribute to a national river. The *Penshurst* belonged to the old political dispensation, *Cooper's Hill* to the new. As before, Denham showed himself extremely dexterous in calling public attention to his verses; they were full of actuality. He opens by rejecting the habitual appeal to Parnassus and Helicon. To this green hill on the south side of the Thames he cries:—

> "If I can be to thee
> A Poet, thou Parnassus art to me,"

and the stately winding river shall take a nobler place than Helicon. There was a certain manly directness about Denham, which at once recommended him to the public.

In the reprints of his poems which he himself issued, and in those which have since been standard, the tone of *Cooper's Hill* is rigidly Royalist. But a glance at the very rare first edition of 1642[1], shows that the author revised almost every other line, and omitted whole passages which proved him to lean towards the Neuters. At present the sudden reference to St Paul's, and the eulogy of Waller, follow the invocation very abruptly. In 1642 these were led up to by some curious lines, the appropriateness of which when Waller's plot was discovered a few months later on, must have made Denham's ears tingle and his hair stand on end:—

> "Some study plots, and some those plots to undo,
>   Others to make them and undo them too,
>   False to their hopes, afraid to be secure,
>   Those mischiefs only which they make, endure;

[1] "Cooper's Hill. A Poeme. London. Printed for Tho. Walkley, and are to be sold at his shop at the Signe of the Flying Horse between York House and Britain's Burse. 1642." Tho. Walkley was the printer of Waller's first genuine edition.

> Blinded of light, and sick of being well,
> In tumult seek their peace, their heaven in hell."

Of course Denham intended no reference to his friend's projects, of which he probably knew nothing; his mysterious allusions are doubtless to such double dealings as Hotham's conduct, with regard to the proposed capitulation of Hull. Our author's most extraordinary indiscretion, however, occurs at the close of the first edition, which ended with these lines :—

> "Therefore their boundless power let Princes draw
> Within the channel and the shores of law,
> And may that law, which teaches Kings to sway
> Their sceptres, teach their subjects to obey."

This was the very doctrine of the Neuters, and cannot have given Charles I. any satisfaction, if a copy of his servant's poem came into his hands as he sat down in a passion to the beleaguerment of Gloucester.

The passage by which *Cooper's Hill* is best known, consists of four lines which I cannot resist the pleasure of now once more repeating. He says to the Thames, which he has been praising above Eridanus and Pactolus :—

> "O could I flow like thee, and make thy stream
> My great example, as it is my theme!

Though deep, yet clear, though gentle, yet not dull,
Strong without rage, without o'erflowing full."

These are marvellous lines; they are among the memories of our language; and if Sir John Denham had been habitually lifted on this graceful and pure level of eloquence, most later poets, at all events those of his own order, might have addressed to him the same adroit compliment. But there exists a mystery about these lines. In collating the first edition I was amazed to find them entirely absent, and they do not occur until the second edition of the poem, published in 1643. Their place is taken until then by a quaint and rather silly promise that the waters of Thames, in reward for their exemplary behaviour in the neighbourhood of Chertsey and Egham,

"Shall visit Jove's abodes
To shine amongst the stars, and bathe the Gods."

Nor is the versification of the poem in any other instance so fine and regular as in the celebrated quatrain, which, for want of better information, we must continue to consider the most brilliant example of second thoughts in the English language.

On the whole, there are few poems which have enjoyed so great and so sustained a reputation as *Cooper's Hill*, which so little respond to it in the eyes of a modern reader[1]. Yet we must not lose sight of the fact that its fame *was* sustained, and seek to discover the cause. Long after Cowley, Davenant, and their crew had sunk into neglect, Denham and Waller preserved their reputation unassailed. Prior asserts their importance, as the two pioneers of our poetry. Pope and Garth, who represented the extremity of critical acumen in an age which had begun to look without prejudice on the founders of its own fashions, spoke out clearly in praise of Denham. The *Windsor Forest* of the one and the *Claremont* of the other were direct imitations of *Cooper's Hill,* written no less than seventy years after its publication[2]. "On Cooper's Hill," says Pope, moved to unusual enthusiasm,

"On Cooper's Hill eternal wreaths shall grow
While lasts the mountain, or while Thames shall flow."

To comprehend all this, we must, in the first place, acknowledge the genuine force and sinew of

---

[1] It would seem that Denham's ear was imperfect, though I confess I have not been able to convict him of that pravity in riming of which Johnson accused him.

[2] Perhaps the latest tribute of unmitigated praise, is Somerville's, in the third book of *The Chace,* 1735:—

"tread, with respectful awe,
Windsor's green glades, where Denham, tuneful bard,
Charm'd once the list'ning Dryads with his song,
Sublimely sweet."

Denham's rugged poem. There is sound thought in it, carefully expressed, without adornment or choice of melody, in successive blows of the sledge-hammer. After this sort of writing had once been conceived, it was comparatively easy to improve upon it, to give regularity to the stroke, grace and ease to the movement. The praise of having invented, or at least having been the first to employ in a sustained effort, a new form of English poetry must always insure Denham a niche in the history of our literature.

In this same year, 1643, an event occurred which attracted little notice in those dreadful years. The Civil War had broken out, and in the west one by one the parliamentary towns were falling into the hands of the King's generals. But late in the summer one handsome and gallant young fellow, riding down the deep-leaved lanes that led from Dartmoor into the little ancient borough of Chagford, at the head of a troop of the King's horse, met a party of Roundheads at the entrance of the town, and was cut down and killed. This was Sidney Godolphin, the hope of a great house, a courtier, a scholar, and a poet as well as a brave soldier.

We may search in vain for the Poems of Sidney Godolphin. Waller, who had been his friend and master in the art of verse, preserved a few of them, and others are to be picked up here and there by accident; but they never have been collected, in that day or in this. He died too young to win a place in literature, and he formed merely one more precious sacrifice laid on the vast altar of Charles I.'s stupid and obstinate pride. But if he had lived he would have won a name for himself. He was the first young man clearly to see what it was that Waller wished to do in modification of our national prosody, and his thin remains are singularly ripe and strangely free from all romantic influence. He had moved in the circle of Waller's friends at Lees and at Penshurst, and like Waller, he had written verses on the untimely death of the beautiful Lady Rich, Sacharissa's cousin. Here are some of these verses, which Elijah Fenton found and printed in 1729:—

"Possess'd of all that nature could bestow,
　All we can wish to be, or reach to know:
　Equal to all the patterns which our mind
　Can frame of good, beyond the good we find:
　All beauties which have pow'r to bless the sight,
　Mix'd with transparent virtue's greater light,
　At once producing love, and reverence,
　The admiration of the soul, and sense;
　The most discerning thoughts; the calmest breast,
　Most apt to pardon, needing pardon least;

> The largest mind, and which did most extend
> To all the laws of daughter, wife, and friend;
> The most allow'd example, by what line
> To live; what path to follow; what decline;
> Who best all distant virtues reconcil'd,
> Strict, cheerful, humble, great, severe, and mild;
> Constantly pious to her latest breath,
> Not more a pattern in her life than death,
> The Lady Rich lies here! More frequent tears
> Have never honour'd any tomb, than Hers."

There is perhaps a touch of the old-fashioned method of versification in the final couplet. The remainder is sustained at a far more even height of eloquence, and in neater couplets than Denham could at that time pretend to have reached, and it is probable that if Godolphin had lived, his executive skill in verse would have hastened the coming of the Augustan era.

The date, 1643, then, is a very important one in our whole inquiry. It has hitherto been rashly presumed that it was the Exile, which by bringing the poets to Paris, and placing them in contact with the French masters of literature, brought about the Classical reaction. But if I have been able to prove anything it is this, that the Exile had not taken place, that not a single Royalist writer had come under the French influence, when that reaction had already begun, and had even advanced to a certain point of development. The year 1643 gives us the opportunity of exactly gauging what had been done; it is the date of Waller's flight, of Sidney Godolphin's death, of Denham's publication of his *Cooper's Hill* revised; and we see that before the Exile began each of these important writers had finished the most characteristic part of his works, that part which the critics of the coming age were principally to point to as his respective contribution to the change. Two of them were to write much more, and Denham, at least, was to write with considerably more of the Gallic grace, but no one who reads their early pieces can doubt the direction their talent was spontaneously taking. The Revolution swept them over to France, and there there was much for them to learn; but the great point upon which I desire to insist is that before they started they knew as clearly as possible what it was they wished for. French taste and practice merely provided them with a primrose path up the prim and dusty Helicon which they had long determined to climb.

It is extremely difficult to follow the fortunes of literature through the vicissitudes of the Civil War. In order to do so with some measure of success we must fix our attention on the movements of Queen Henrietta Maria. Several of the most important men of letters were entirely devoted to her service. We shall see, later on, what part she gave to Davenant in her first visit to France. When she fled from Exeter with the newborn Princess of Wales in July, 1644, Cowley was with her, and for the next twelve years was constantly attached to her person. Another interesting figure in letters took part in that doleful flight, namely, Margaret Lucas, the girl who was to become the most eccentric of all poetasters, the erudite and fantastic Duchess of Newcastle. The Queen settled for three months at the baths of Bourbon, whither, to soothe her misery, as Madame de Motteville tells us, Anne of Austria sent her sympathetic messages, and a nurse, and 20,000 pistoles. She passed on for the winter to Paris, and hither the young Duke of Newcastle, flying from defeat at Marston Moor, joined her, swiftly to be smitten by the lettered charms of Margaret Lucas. There was presently a colony of English people in Paris. Hobbes, the philosopher and critic, Leviathan himself, was already there, and the last of the great Jacobean dramatists, James Shirley, who had left a starving wife and children behind him, was in attendance upon the Royal Mistress who had been his consistent patron.

Well might Cowley speak with bitterness of "us, the poets militant below." As he walked in the streets of Paris, he met his old friend Crashaw starving, and had but just enough patronage left to find him a place in the household of a Roman cardinal, where he might eat a piece of bread. Killigrew, wearily wasting the vigour of his youth in secret missions to all the courts of Europe, came back each time more wretched, with a dismaller tale to tell. Yet, at worst, the poets in exile, with all their poverty and discomfort, fared better than the poets at home[1]. The first great loss which letters and statecraft suffered was when Lord Falkland fell, on the 20th of September, 1643, at the Battle of Newbury. He called for a clean shirt before he went into battle, for, said he, "They shall not find my dead body in foul linen." And as his friends begged him, a civilian, not to rush into a needless danger, he bid them know that he was weary of the times, and believed he should be out of it all ere night. He was; and with him

---

[1] Denham says of Killigrew, William Murray and himself:—

"Mirth makes us not mad,
Nor sobriety sad,
But of that we are seldom in danger;
At Paris, at Rome,
At the Hague, we're at home,
The Good Fellow is nowhere a stranger."

fell the greatest ornament of the Royalist party, the man from whom more might have been expected than from any other soldier or civilian in all the King's party, that almost fabulous Cary, Viscount Falkland, of whom Clarendon, as the mouthpiece of the times, says, that he "was a person of such prodigious parts of learning and knowledge, of that inimitable sweetness and delight in conversation, and so flowing and obliging a humanity and goodness to mankind, and of that primitive simplicity and integrity of life, that if there were no other brand upon this odious and accursed civil war, than that single loss, it must be most infamous and execrable to all posterity." The body in which so much wit, virtue, and energy resided was small and feeble; those who knew him noted the brightness of his black eyes; Mr Matthew Arnold, in a most striking essay, has drawn attention recently to his intellectual character.

Lord Falkland was the centre of the group of wits to which Waller, Morley, and Godolphin belonged, and we should expect him, with his liberal and sympathetic character, to be with them in their literary revolution. But, on the contrary, the existing poems of Lord Falkland belong entirely to the old school, with frequent use of overflow, and with the accent shifting from place to place in successive lines. If we had space for such comparisons, it would not be uninteresting to place side by side an exercise of Lord Falkland's and one of Sidney Godolphin's, each in heroic couplet, by way of emphasizing the distinction between the two styles; but we may remark, in passing, that the men who showed the truest aptitude for the new manner of writing appeared scarcely to have learnt, but to be born into it.

Meanwhile Falkland was not the only poet who did not bear his life away from the battle fields of the Civil War. Peter Hausted, a Cambridge clergyman, who wrote one remarkable play, *The Rival Friends*, was shot on the ramparts of Banbury, while the Roundheads were vigorously besieging it in 1645, and he lies buried in Banbury Church. Fanshawe had been made tutor to the Prince of Wales, and fled with him from Exeter to Scilly, thence to Jersey, and placed him at last, in 1646, in the hands of his mother in Paris, after infinite toil and alarm by land and sea. Cleveland, the forerunner of Hudibras, had, perhaps, the hardest fate of all, for, although he was by no means a fanatical supporter of the King's extreme views, he left Cambridge for Oxford to wait upon Charles, helped to defend Newark through the assault and siege of that town, and avoided no hardship of the war, until at last he was taken prisoner and thrown into jail at Yarmouth, where he languished for years, until Oliver Cromwell released him in consideration of his literary gifts and his political helplessness.

Most of the leading men of letters, however, and in particular those in whom we now take an interest, escaped to France. All the English exiles were well received, for the sake of Henrietta Maria, who was a very great favourite, even with the common people. We may read in the *Mémoires* of Madame de Motteville how inconsolable, how like a draggled and bespattered bird of gorgeous plumage, the Queen of England seemed at first, and how, slowly, as one of her children after another was restored to her, she preened her feathers, and regained something of her sanguine composure. We read of the fêtes at Fontainebleau in the summer of 1646, and again in 1647; of the urbane affability of Anne of Austria and of the good manners of little Louis XIV., of the "balls, comedies and promenades" with which the English exiles were regaled, and in the reading of all this we must interpolate for our present entertainment that among those exiles were some of the brightest Englishmen then living—probably Waller and

Hobbes, certainly Cowley, Fanshawe, Shirley, and Davenant.

What, then, were the influences which were exercised on these men's minds by their exchange of London and Oxford for Paris and Fontainebleau? On some of them we may safely say, There was none at all. Sir Richard Fanshawe, for instance, a learned and industrious poet of the third order, was about thirty-eight years of age when he conducted the future Charles II. to France. On him France had no effect whatever. His famous translation of the *Pastor Fido*, published in 1647, his little epic of *Dido and Æneas* in the Spenserian stanza, his odes and sonnets, his epistles and addresses, are all of them in the full-blown Marinist manner of the preceding generation. Here is an example of a pretty stanza in praise of peace:—

> "Plant trees you may, and see them shoot
>   Up with your children, to be served
> To your clean boards, and the fair'st fruit
>   To be preserved,
> And learn to use their several gums;
>   'Tis innocence in the sweet blood
> Of cherries, apricots, and plums
>   To be imbrued."

Not a line of this but Waller or Denham would

have rejected. It was precisely these dislocated constructions, these languid broken rhythms, these harsh clusters of consonants that it was their function to rebel against. And yet, for a Marinist stanza of the school of 1630, it is distinctly pretty.

To men like Shirley and Fanshawe, then, France had no lesson; but what did it say to the reformers, to the men whose ears were open? The posthumous poems of Malherbe, could they be without interest to Waller? Is it credible that the relation of Chapelain's odes and St Amant's anacreontics to the anacreontics and odes of Cowley is purely accidental? I think not. The condition of French literature was precisely that which was likely to discourage the romantic and Spanish tendencies in our poets, and to encourage the feeling for classical precision. Some wit said that French poetry in the age of Anne of Austria was a young lady, no longer quite young, who had missed two or three advantageous marriages, and who, in order not to die a maid, accepted the hand of M. de Malherbe, an elderly gentleman. We might, perhaps, say that English poetry was a widow, who had married Shakespeare for love, and now consented to marry Waller for a position. The state of things was so exactly analogous that the lady from the north could learn much by the experience of her slightly older sister.

But, to descend from this too oriental region of simile, the parallelism between the history of French and English poetry of precision is in one particular so exact that I wonder that it has not been, as I believe it has not, already observed. The sweet and monotonous versification of Malherbe was first of all emulated by his pupil Maynard, whose slightly provincial vein of reflection was expressed with a more rugged vigour than Malherbe had displayed. Exactly the same language might be used to describe the relation of Waller to Denham, and the latter, with his slight touch of provinciality, from which the former is free, and with his force of versification, would be singularly like Maynard, even if it were not the case that the principal poems of them both—the *Cooper's Hill* and the *Alcippe*—are occupied by precisely the same order of reflections, and might each, in parts, be a paraphrase of the other. It would be exceedingly rash to take for granted that Maynard ever heard of Denham, or *vice versâ;* such a supposition, indeed, is extremely improbable; but the same ideas were common to both, and it seems to me beyond a doubt that by transplanting English poetry into French air we encouraged the growth of that particular branch of it which was in sympathy with France.

It would be interesting to know, it is possibly within the bounds of research to discover, what plays were performed at Fontainebleau to dissolve the sad thoughts of Henrietta Maria and to amuse her silent children. The *Menteur* of Corneille belongs to that year, 1646. It is not to be doubted that amateurs of verse, such as were so many of the English exiles, would follow with interest what the great Corneille was doing with the alexandrine, how he was polishing it, and learning to direct it like a javelin, ponderous, invertible, lethal. This was what English verse had to learn to become. Denham had caught the notion of the clean, self-sustaining verse in his Corneille-like

"Strong without rage, without o'erflowing full,"

and Dryden was to carry on the discovery with a sullen majesty that was all his own.

"Like a wedge in a block, ringed to the bar,"

had seemed a sufficiently melodious example of five-foot iambic verse to Donne and the Marinists. It still seemed good enough to Fanshawe and Shirley. It had never seemed good enough to Waller and Denham. Cowley and Davenant first awoke to a sense of its insufficiency on their arrival in France. In this summary we may say that we hold the theme of these lectures in a nutshell.

We saw in our last discourse that Waller, detected in a serious plot, contrived by the exercise of great adroitness, and, I am afraid we must add, great hypocrisy, to escape to France alive in 1643. To buy his release he had to sell estates which produced a rental of £1,000 a year. With part of this money he probably fled, for it seems that his mother—who continued to live at Beaconsfield, and to nurse the property, as she had done before, when her son was a child,—was not allowed to send him any remittances. This, at all events, was the story, and Waller took care to give out that he was living entirely on the sale of his wife's jewels. As he kept open table in Paris for ten years, and was the only English exile except Lord Jermyn, Henrietta Maria's second husband, who could afford to do so, and as he certainly was in much more luxurious circumstances than the queen herself, we may be allowed to doubt this.

Old Mrs Waller at Beaconsfield seems to have been a lady of great astuteness. Like her son, she was an adept in the art of trimming, and while remaining at heart a Royalist, she made capital of her relationships as the sister of Hampden and cousin of Cromwell. The Protector used to visit at her house, and it is said that once, at her table, she ventured to tease him so far with predictions of his political downfall, that he suddenly threw his napkin over her head to silence her. Later on, it would appear, her tongue began to wag still more freely, for not only did Cromwell cease to visit her, but he forbade her to leave her house at Beaconsfield. But these comfortable visits to the mother, and horseplay with napkins at cosy little dinners, may perhaps serve to account for the fact that Waller kept his head on his shoulders in 1643.

My eminent friend Prof. Gardiner is just about to deal with this year in detail, and I expect that his researches will throw fresh light upon Waller's plot. We saw that he freely denounced everybody he could think of as an accomplice; even the great Selden was one of his victims. Nevertheless, as Clarendon has noted, he was not ostracized among the Royalist party for what looks to us like boundless and cowardly treachery. Yet there was no tendency to overlook such conduct in others. For a much less shameful temporizing than this, Barton Holiday, the author of *Technogamia*, was rancorously attacked by his own party, and never forgiven. I expect that the accusations of Waller were chiefly against persons wholly out of the power of the Parliamentarians, and that his party recognized that there had been more cry than wool in his boisterous confessions. No reflections were made against him, at all events, and nobody avoided him. He went to Rouen, married a second wife, and seems to have resided two years there. His favourite daughter, Margaret, who became his amanuensis, was born in Rouen.

In 1645, while he was in Rouen, he published his poems. The bibliography of Waller is rather obscure, but it seems that of the three editions which appeared, under the names of three different booksellers, in that year, the first was a mere piracy, the second published with the author's consent, and the third a theft emboldened by the poet's enforced absence from home[1]. The instant success of all three editions testifies to the interest

---

[1] The editions of 1645 may thus be distinguished:

a. "Printed for T. Walkley." This is the first spurious edition, "the adulterate Copy, surreptitiously and illegally imprinted, to the derogation of the Author and the abuse of the Buyer."

b. "Printed by T. W. for Humphrey Mosley." With a preface signed E. W. This seems to be genuine. It consists of pp. 92, carried on to p. 111 by insertion of "Mr Waller's Speeches in Parliament," after which, in the copy which I possess, is added an appendix to the poems, paged 93—96, and containing, among other pieces, "Love's Farewell," "On a Girdle," and "To Chloris."

c. "Printed by J. N. for H. Moseley." These three simultaneous editions satisfied public curiosity until 1664.

that Waller's reputation had excited, and the readiness with which his experiments in versification were received. He was forty years of age when this first issue of his poems was published[1], and we may remember that it was also in 1645, and at an age almost as mature, that Milton came forward for the first time with a collection of poems. There exists a portrait of Waller from this same year, first engraved for Fenton's edition; it represents him in a heavy, dark periwig, with clean-shaven face, the whole style that of the new age, the age of Louis XIV. The likeness must have been a good one, for in the close, discreet lips, the handsome but somewhat furtive eyes, and the ill-shapen nose, there is more individuality than a flattering painter would affect.

It seems probable that in the winter of 1645 Waller broke up his establishment at Rouen, and settled his wife and children in Paris, while he went for the winter to Italy. In March, 1646, John Evelyn found him at Venice, and persuaded him to be his travelling companion. In company with "Mr Waller the celebrated poet," a Mr Abdy, and one Captain Wray, Evelyn set forth on Easter Monday, and we are able to follow Waller in his friend's diary for the next six months. He waited

[1] Appendix III.

in the coach below, while Evelyn took leave of the dying Earl of Arundel, and then the four gentlemen drove away to Vicenza. Here they found, at once, that they had one person in their company who was distasteful to the others. Captain Wray, besides being the son of a pestilent Roundhead, "minded," says Evelyn, "nothing save drinking and folly," and was for hurrying them on whenever they wished to stop and enjoy pictures or statues. At Lodi, Evelyn strayed from his companions, and was caught peeping at the governor of the city, who was being shaved; and was only just in time to run like a schoolboy through the streets to the Jesuits' church, where Waller and the others were, and to succeed, when the Swiss guard arrived, in looking as though he knew nothing about governors or peeping.

At Milan, Dr Ferrarius carried them in his coach to see the Borromean Library, and here took place the terrible incident, which Evelyn graphically describes, in which a hospitable Scots Colonel, at the close of a sumptuous dinner which he gave them, must needs show them his stable, and mounting a beautiful horse against the advice of his groom, was crushed to death before their eyes by the creature viciously rearing with him against the wall. Next day they hastened to be gone, and made their way to Lake Maggiore, up to the head of which they sailed, and then ascended the Alps, "through strange, horrid, and fearful crags and tracts." There was never a writer who was less in sympathy with Alpine scenery, we may be sure, than Waller. At the village of Simplon, Captain Wray, who was constantly vexing the quiet souls of the other three travellers, got into a real scrape. He had brought a water-spaniel from England, "a huge, filthy cur," says Evelyn, and this beast amused itself by hunting a herd of goats down a gully into a stream. One goat, at least, was drowned, and next morning when the English party started they were set upon by the inhabitants, were beaten and imprisoned. Their sorrows were great, and when at last they reached the valley of the Rhone, their hearts sang within them. To cross the Alps in those days was certainly no holiday-task.

It is not necessary for us to follow the friends closely in their travels, especially as Waller seems to have done nothing remarkable, not even by making himself disagreeable or by keeping a water-spaniel. At Martigny Evelyn made a remark which has been attributed to various later wits, and in particular to Rogers, namely, that one lusty Swiss could keep the gate of the Valais against an army. At Geneva the other three waited for Evelyn to sicken of the small-pox, and to recover of it. Waller would seem to have beguiled the tedium of nearly two months' idleness by conversing with the famous Genevese scholar, Dr Diodati. It seems odd that, as he could really be of no service to Evelyn, he did not push on at once for Paris. It was July before the travellers went to Lyons, whence they proceeded to Roanne. They lay in that town in damask beds, and "felt like emperors," and there it occurred to them to do a very picturesque and unusual thing. Instead of posting through the plains of France, they determined to sail down the Loire to Orleans; they chartered a boat, and performed the voyage in two days, taking turns to row, and it seems to have been a very charming little finale to their long tour. Evelyn says:—

"Sometimes we footed it through pleasant fields and meadows; sometimes we shot at fowls, and other birds. [This shooting at fowls was a little hazardous.] Nothing came amiss: sometimes we played at cards, whilst others sung, or were composing verses; for had we not the great poet, Mr Waller, in our company."

Waller now seems to have settled at Paris. In 1647 he was at St Valéry, probably for some political purpose, to be near the English coast, for his home undoubtedly was at Paris until 1653, when he petitioned Cromwell to let him return to England and was allowed to do so. The poem which he wrote on that occasion, although far too fulsome to come with propriety from a man in his political position and of his antecedents, contains some interesting writing. Here is a passage in which, when we take into account the exaggerated strain of panegyric then universally indulged in, we may find a just appreciation of what Cromwell had done to raise the prestige of England among the nations of the Continent. It will also show us that Waller had carried the refining and polishing of his versification to a still higher pitch during his ten years in France.

"Lords of the world's great waste, the ocean, we
  Whole forests send to reign upon the sea;
  And ev'ry coast may trouble, or relieve:
  But none can visit us without your leave.
  Angels, and we, have this prerogative,
  That none can at our happy seats arrive:
  While we descend at pleasure, to invade
  The bad with vengeance, and the good to aid.
  Our little world, the image of the great,
  Like that, amidst the boundless ocean set,

Of her own growth, hath all that nature craves;
And all that's rare, as tribute from the waves.
As Egypt does not on the clouds rely,
But to the Nile owes more than to the sky;
So, what our earth, and what our heav'n, denies,
Our ever-constant friend, the sea, supplies.
The taste of hot Arabia's spice we know,
Free from the scorching sun, that makes it grow:
Without the worm, in Persian silks we shine;
And, without planting, drink of ev'ry wine.
To dig for wealth we weary not our limbs;
Gold, tho' the heaviest metal, hither swims:
Ours is the harvest where the Indians mow,
We plough the deep, and reap what others sow.
Things of the noblest kind our own soil breeds;
Stout are our men, and warlike are our steeds:
Rome, tho' her eagle thro' the world had flown,
Could never make this Island all her own."

Denham's career during the Commonwealth was a very different one from Waller's. At the breaking out of the Civil War an attempt was made to turn him into a soldier. He was sent as Governor of Farnham Castle to hold that fortress for the King; but he was a failure there, and retired for a while into obscurity. He seems to have followed Charles about from place to place, and he tells us that one morning, when he waited upon the King in the garden at Caversham, his Majesty smiled and said that he could give him news of himself, for that he had just seen some verses of his. The verses[1] were those prefixed in 1647, to Fanshawe's *Pastor Fido*, a presentation copy of which had probably just reached the King. Charles seems to have been very unsympathetic about them: perhaps he had no great idea of Denham's ability in other matters. He told him, in terms which must have been very galling to the author of *Cooper's Hill*, that he liked the verses well, but he would advise him to write no more, "for that when men are young and have little else to do, they may vent the outcomings of their fancy in that way, but when they are thought fit for more serious employments, if they still persisted in that course, it would look as if they minded not the way to any better."

It is a little odd that Denham himself was the person who informed the world of this royal reprimand; the reason possibly was that he might remind Charles II., to whom he addressed these remarks in 1667, of the "serious employment" he

---

[1] Four of them are worth quoting:—
    A new and nobler way thou dost pursue
    To make translations, and translators too;
    They but preserve the ashes, thou the flame,
    True to his sense, but truer to his fame.

had been entrusted with in 1647, namely, the being charged by the Queen with a private message to Charles I., who was then at St James's. Denham stayed with the King, until in November the latter made his escape from Hampton Court. Denham remained in London, and in April, 1648, after the civil war had broken out anew, he managed to steal from the Earl of Northumberland his royal charge the Duke of York, then a boy of fifteen. It would seem from what Clarendon and others say of this flight of James, who was dressed as a girl, and had great difficulty in reaching Middelburg without discovery, that Denham's share in effecting his escape was less than the poet afterward reported it to be.

He seems, however, to have gained a reputation for diplomacy, for soon after the execution of the King, he was sent from Paris, in company with William, Lord Crofts, to collect money in Poland from Scotch people settled in that country, and with such extraordinary success that he brought £10,000 back with him. He made a doggerel poem about this expedition, in which he gives us no very clear account of what occurred on the occasion. He wrote very little more verse until the Restoration. He pretends that he took that remark of His Majesty's in the garden at Caversham so much to heart that he never felt any inclination to write again; but that, of course, is nonsense[1]. He probably found that his vein, which never flowed very freely, had run dry. It gushed again before he died, as we shall see. His best poem written during the Exile is one " Against Love," which is inspired by a sort of spirited cynicism, very paradoxical and fantastic, but rather refreshing after the interminable love-languishings and melting sonnets to my lady's eyebrow which had constituted the main part of lyrical literature in the preceding generation. I will close the present chapter by printing a few of these stanzas, the versification of which appears to me to be particularly forcible and graceful:

"AGAINST LOVE.

Love making all things else his foes,
Like a fierce torrent overflows
Whatever doth his course oppose.

This was the cause the poets sung,
Thy Mother from the sea was sprung,
But they were mad to make thee young.

---

[1] He had forgotten that in the very next year, 1648, he had published a paraphrase of *Cato Major on Old Age*. Was it modesty at the Royal reprimand, or a desire to seem consistent, which made him omit this poem in 1667?

Her father, not her son, art thou;
From our desires our actions grow,
And from the cause the effect must flow.

Love is as old as place or time;
'Twas he the fatal tree did climb,
Grandsire of Father Adam's crime.

Love drowsy days and stormy nights
Makes, and breaks friendship, whose delights
Feed, but not glut our appetites.

How happy he, that loves not, lives!
Him neither hope nor fear deceives
To Fortune who no hostage gives.

How unconcerned in things to come!
If here he frets, he finds at Rome,
At Paris, or Madrid his home.

Secure from low and private ends,
His life, his zeal, his wealth attends
His prince, his country and his friends."

DAVENANT AND COWLEY.

DAVENANT AND COWLEY.

IT is very important that we should appreciate the temper of mind in which it is desirable to approach literature as distinguished from the history of literature, and still more poetry as distinguished from the history of poetry. Literature, in the exact sense in which I use the word here, is a somewhat rare product. It is the quintessence of good writing, in all ages, in all languages, and no single nation within one single century can be presumed to have supplied very much of it. For instance, this very seventeenth century which we are considering produced of the highest poetic literature, of the literature which is of universal importance, just the writings of Shakespeare and Milton, with some sparse pages from Ben Jonson and Dryden. We look a little closer, with eyes a little less critical, and we see a great deal more than this which is sound poetic literature; we begin to perceive Webster and Herrick, Fletcher and Marvell, Browne and Otway, with a score of lyrists, a score of playwrights, to whom the praise of genuine literary execution, in isolated bursts and fragments, must not be denied. But if we are set upon the discovery of literature alone, and not on the observation of literary history, we must then go no further.

At the present day it is a great temptation to those who have made special periods and segments of the poetic produce of a nation their peculiar care, to exaggerate the value of what they have unearthed. It is human to see exotic beauties in the weed that we ourselves have discovered. But this tendency is one to be avoided, since it is commonly accompanied by an inability to enjoy what is really great in other schools than that in which the education of the taste has been conducted. I have known a scholar, who delighted to excess in Quarles, express an utter contempt for Gray, and another whose taste lay in Occleve confound his own judgment by confessing that he saw nothing praiseworthy in Pope. From this narrowness, from this provincial attitude, which may easily become a snare for those who pursue literature alone, the study of the history of literature may be recommended as an escape.

In this delightful inquiry,—and one of the few pleasant things that Bishop Warburton said, was his remark that the history of literature was the most charming exercise of the human mind,—we are released from the contemplation of the best, and of nothing but the best, from that communion with the quintessence of things which no taste can long endure without feeling a strain, and we are permitted to indulge that curiosity which is excited by the spectacle of motion, of evolution. A writer too crabbed or too insignificant to claim our praise on the score of his verses alone, becomes interesting at once, and important, when we see that he possessed an influence over a younger writer than himself, who attained genuine success, or when he marks a step in the range which culminated at last in a poet.

It is this second attitude of mind which I have to beg from my readers in the whole course of the present argument. From the beginning to the end of it I have been and shall be beset with siren enticements to break away on this side and on that to the fields of genuine literature which lie just beyond our range. I do not deceive myself that there is much literature, of the finer sort, in Waller or in Denham, and I am about to introduce an author in whom I should be almost inclined to say that there is none at all. It would be refreshing to close such books as *Madagascar* and *Gondibert*, and listen to those Dorian strains from Milton's oaten stop, which were making the solitudes of Horton vocal. But literature just now is not our pursuit, but the history of literature, and, paradoxical as it may be, in the development of English poetical taste in the middle of the seventeenth century, Milton took a part decidedly less prominent than Davenant.

We have already acquainted ourselves with the pioneers of the classical transition, with Waller and with Denham. Next in honour after these names were quoted, when the transition was complete, those of Davenant and Cowley. The peculiarity in the position of these two latter poets lay in the fact that they were both of them, but Davenant especially, perverts from the older romantic school. Waller, as we have seen, was born with a curious gift for distich, and carefully held himself aloof from the men of the age into which he was bred, and Denham more or less did the same. They had to struggle against adverse fashion, but that struggle was all without. Davenant, on the other hand, was nurtured in the very heart of romance; we shall see that he had deliberately to unlearn all he had learned, to wean himself from all he had loved. It is possible that the reason why his defection to the classical camp was considered such a triumph, and why his poems excited so much adverse criticism, was because he was felt to be a prize, no common soldier or townsman, but a princeling born in the purple.

There are few things more exasperating than the tendency which abides in the gossipy human tongue to spoil a pretty story, which is true, by embroidering upon it a scandalous story, which is not true. The legend which makes Shakespeare the actual father of William Davenant[1], obscures the really charming relations which existed between that hero's parents and the greatest of poets. This legend recurs so frequently, and is so often rather attacked from its unpleasantness than confuted as history, that we may spare a few minutes for its examination. In France it is so much delighted in, that no account of English literature is complete without it, and a living playwright has made it the subject of a drama, which the French company brought to London in its repertory, and acted in compliment to our nation. The real truth about Davenant's childhood, then, as far as we can make it out, is this.

[1] I see no reason for retaining the spelling "D'Avenant," or "D'avenant," which the poet occasionally affected. The ancient family from which he claimed to spring, the Davenants of Sible Hedingham, knew no such refinement, nor did the illustrious Bishop of Salisbury. His father, the vintner, signs his will "John Davenentt."

In coming up to London from Stratford, Shakespeare was accustomed to call at the Crown Tavern, in Oxford, which was kept by Mr John Davenant, vintner, a respectable and wealthy citizen, who afterwards rose to be Mayor of Oxford, and who possessed an unusual taste for plays, playwrights, and everything connected with acting. He was a grave and melancholy man, but his gravity was tempered by the vivacity of his wife, who was noticeably handsome[1]. This couple, of whose mutual affection and loyalty we have contemporary evidence, had a family of seven children during the last years of Shakespeare's life. The eldest of these, the Rev. Robert Davenant, grew up to be a commonplace clergyman, of whom only one interesting thing is recorded. When he was an old man, somewhere in the third quarter of the century, he was asked if he had known Shakespeare. "Ay," he answered, "and he hath kissed me a hundred times[2]." Curious to think of this old clerical gentleman whose only interest to us or

---

[1] Anthony à Wood says: Davenant's "mother was a very beautiful woman, of a good wit and conversation, in which she was imitated by none of her children but by this William." *Ath. Oxon.* ii. col. 411.

[2] Aubrey. This Robert Davenant was a Fellow of St John's College, Oxford, and became chaplain to John Davenant, the Bishop of Salisbury.

to anyone is that, when he was a child, Shakespeare had kissed him.

On such intimate terms was the great man with this family; and what could be more natural than that he should stand godfather, as he did, to the next son, William, our poet? On the 3rd of March, 1606, this interesting ceremonial took place, in the church of St Martin's at Oxford. It seems that Shakespeare remained on a familiar footing with the family until his death in 1616, and there can be no doubt that he had instilled a love of poetry into the mind of his godchild, for the very first verses which Davenant wrote, at the age of eleven, were those composing the "Ode in Remembrance of Master William Shakespeare," which we find appended to his *Madagascar*. This ode is of no use to us; it is crammed with effete and monstrous conceits, but contains no single crumb of autobiographical evidence. Presently, in 1622, the mother, Mrs Davenant, died, and her husband only survived her a few days, pined away, and was buried in the same grave.

This pleasant story about Shakespeare and his Oxford friends would probably have come down to us unspoiled if it had not been for the tattling monkey-tongue of Pope. Oldys, the antiquary, sitting beside Pope at the dinner-table of the Earl of Oxford, was regaled by him with the story, that one day little William Davenant, being met madly flying from school down the street at Oxford, was caught and stopped by an elderly townsman, who wished to know whither he was posting in that heat and hurry. "To see my godfather, Master Shakespeare." "That's a good boy," said the old man, "but have a care of taking God's name in vain." Naturally all the company at Lord Oxford's asked Pope where he found this story, and he immediately quoted Betterton as his authority. Mr Betterton, the player, he said, who had known Davenant intimately, had told him the story, and himself believed it. It was then noticed that the gossipy and delightful Aubrey, who had been a still greater ally of Davenant's, had recorded that when that poet was among his familiar friends he was in the habit of appealing to them to know whether he did not write as befitted Shakespeare's son. This was thereupon taken as proving that Davenant himself believed and delighted in the story, for the eighteenth century had forgotten the seventeenth-century custom of calling the pupils or enthusiastic imitators of a poet his sons. When Davenant made this boast to Butler and other friends, he evidently meant no more than to claim such kinship with Shakespeare as Randolph,

Herrick, and Cartwright claimed with Ben Jonson.

We may therefore dismiss the legend; but we must remember that it was no legend that young William Davenant was the godson and pet of Shakespeare, the only child, indeed, with whose first buddings of talent the patronage of that great name can be identified. This was his first romantic distinction; his second was only just a little less distinguished, namely, his association with Fulke Greville, Lord Brooke. He left Lincoln College, Oxford, where he was an undergraduate, and went up to town soon after the death of his parents in 1622. His father had wished him to be apprenticed to a City merchant, but the boy successfully avoided this, and secured an easier appointment. He was made page to the Duchess of Richmond, and traces of his stay with this fashionable and superstitious great lady have been discovered in his plays.

From her service he passed, probably about 1624, into that of one of the most interesting minor personages of the day, Lord Brooke. This was a stately old relic from the beautiful days of Elizabeth, the last of all the clan that had sung her praises. He had been the bosom-friend of Sir Philip Sidney; and he and Sir Edward Dyer, who had himself now been dead for nearly twenty years, had held the pall at the funeral of that beloved and immortal poet. In the person of Fulke Greville, poet, statesman, and soldier, and eminent in all three professions, the chivalry of the era of the Maiden Queen found its last harbour. He was the Sir Bedivere of that romantic Court of the virgin Star of the North, who sat, as he himself had said, with

"The red and white rose quartered in her face."

That Davenant should be received under the personal patronage of such a man, was tantamount to saying that he was received into the penetralia of what remained of the great romantic school[1]. In his own abstruse, but weighty and dignified poetry, Lord Brooke combined, with the old Sidneian sweetness, an ingenuity of phrase, an intellectual and fanciful, rather than a sensual and imaginative element, which really stepped over the Marinists, and linked the Elizabethans with the classical school. In other words, his poetry strongly affected Davenant, and, through him, the school itself. We shall presently see how important a place the poem of *Gondibert* holds in the history

---

[1] So Edward Hyde, afterwards Lord Clarendon, reminds him in the childish verses prefixed to *Albovine* in 1629:—

"Thy wit hath purchas'd such a Patron's name
To deck thy front, etc."

of this classical transition; and nothing appears to me to be more plain than the effect which the versification as well as the matter and manner of Lord Brooke's dramatic pamphlets had upon *Gondibert*, although the latter was written a quarter of a century after his death.

It is, therefore, not unfitting that we should dwell a little upon Lord Brooke's relations with Davenant, who was his companion until the latter was three-and-twenty years of age. It was at Lord Brooke's house that Davenant began to work seriously at poetic art. I do not think it has been hitherto noticed that one of Davenant's plays, *The Cruel Brother*, was licensed by the Master of the Revels in January, 1627, that is to say, nearly two years before Lord Brooke was murdered. This terrible event, which would have excited interest as one of the most sensational crimes of the day, even if the victim had been a less illustrious and public personage, took place on the 1st of September, 1628. Lord Brooke, who was seventy-four years of age, lived in considerable state at Brooke House in London, with a little court of retainers around him. He had lately made a will, one of the witnesses to which had been a gentleman-servant, Ralph Haywood by name, who had waited on him for many years. This man, who expected his Lordship to leave him something, cast his eye over the will, and was enraged to find himself not mentioned in it. This preyed on his mind, and he probably became mad. At all events, on the morning of the 1st of September he went to Lord Brooke's bed-chamber as usual, and wakened him; nothing seems to have raised the poet's suspicions; he rose, and Haywood helped him to dress.

Lord Brooke, as an old gentleman of quality, still wore the antiquated costume of the reign of Elizabeth, the trunk-hose and doublet, which had to be fastened together with points when the garments were on. Haywood was stooping behind Lord Brooke, trussing these points, when suddenly, without the least warning, he drew out a knife and stabbed him in the back. At the noise of this, the other servants and attendants, among whom Davenant appears to have been one, hurried to the spot. The murderer, still grasping the knife, rushed into another room, locked himself in, and stabbed himself to death. Lord Brooke lingered for a month, and then died, on the 30th of September, and Davenant was once more thrown upon the world.

He seems to have been taken up at Court, and to have thrown himself upon the stage as a profession. During the next ten years he caused as many of his dramatic productions—tragedies, comedies, and masques—as amounted to ten or twelve to be acted in London, and he grew in the estimation of such influential men as Endymion Porter and Henry Jermyn[1], who introduced him to the notice of the Queen herself. Although he had published nothing but plays, he was selected, in 1637, to succeed Ben Jonson in the distinguished office of poet laureate. Yet these early plays of Davenant's give little excuse for the reputation which their author secured. They are miserable productions, noisy, flashy, insufferably dull. As specimens of versification they are more hopelessly and deliberately faulty than any that had preceded them, and they might almost be suspected of being written to disgust the age with the loose romantic

---

[1] The dedication of *Madagascar*, pretty in itself, and throwing a curious side-light on the mysterious dedication of Shakespeare's *Sonnets*, runs thus:—

IF

THESE POEMS LIVE

MAY

THEIR MEMORIES

BY WHOM

THEY WERE CHERISH'D

END. PORTER, H. JARMYN

LIVE WITH THEM.

prosody, and to force the classical distich on the literature of the country. If Lord Brooke read *The Cruel Brother* or *Albovine*, as it is possible that he did, there could be nothing in either the one or the other to please his severe and super-exquisite taste, and this may perhaps account for the petulance of Davenant in referring to the care with which his master polished and re-polished his own stately periods.

In the year after his appointment to the Laureateship, in 1638, Davenant collected, for the first time, his scattered copies of verses into a volume, which he called *Madagascar*, from the opening poem. Endymion Porter, Suckling, Carew, and Habington, that is to say, the group of Marinist wits who specially flourished just then at the Court of Whitehall, ushered in *Madagascar* with copies of laudatory verses. This piece, which is written in heroic couplets of the old-fashioned kind, is chiefly interesting because it seems to be an imitation of Waller's *Battle of the Summer Islands*, which had probably been written and circulated in MS. a few months earlier; there seems a direct reference to Waller as one

"Whose music might incite
The Swordfish, Thrasher, and the Whale to fight,"

in allusion to the fight with the whales at the end of the *Battle of the Summer Islands*. For the rest, *Madagascar* displays all the faults of Davenant's early style—the absolute want of progression, so that he cannot induce the story to move on at all, the uncouth and broken versification, the intolerable lack of style[1]. The rest of the poems in the volume are better than this opening piece, but none of them are very good. By far the best is this address to Lady Olivia Porter, his friend's wife, which possesses a certain glow and declamatory vigour, not quite unworthy of the page of Fulke Greville and godson of Shakespeare :—

"Go! hunt the whiter ermine, and present
His wealthy skin as this day's tribute sent
To my Endymion's Love; though she be far
More gently smooth, more soft than ermines are.

Go! climb that rock, and when thou there hast found
A star contracted in a diamond,
Give it Endymion's Love, whose lasting eyes
Outlook the starry jewels of the skies.

[1] Or, as Suckling puts it :—

"Since the great Lord of wit,
Donne, parted hence, no man has ever writ
So near him, in his own way."

Go! dive into the southern sea, and when
Thou hast found, to trouble the nice sight of men,
A swelling pearl, and such whose single worth
Boasts all the wonders which the seas bring forth;
Give it Endymion's Love! whose every tear
Would more enrich the skilful jeweller.

How I command! how slowly they obey!
The churlish Tartar will not hunt to-day,
Nor will that lazy sallow Indian strive
To climb the rock, nor that dull negro dive.
Thus poets, like to kings, by trust deceived,
Give oftener what is heard of than received."

We may notice throughout this piece the presence of the old broken prosody, although the verse is particularly good for Davenant. There is as yet in his work no trace of intelligent interest in the innovations of Waller. He was the associate of the Whitehall group of poets, whose work was peculiarly unsympathetic to Waller, and which was destined to be swept away by the first tides of the classical innovation. It would, therefore, have been difficult to find a poet apparently less fit than Davenant to take a part in the new school. He was now thirty-three years of age, and his whole life had been passed in intimate companionship with one after another of the leaders of the romantic party, while, in his own poetry, he had hitherto shown no sign of dissatisfaction with the practice of his masters and his friends. Yet a totally different future was awaiting him; his literary life had really not begun, and he would yet take his place as the third of the renovators of English verse, as they stand in Dryden's list— Waller, Denham, Davenant.

We have little or no record of the process by which Davenant was converted. Politics, diplomacy, and fighting took up a great part of the next twelve years of his life, and when he reappears as a poet, in 1650, the transformation is complete. He puts the last finishing touches to the first volume of his epic poem of *Gondibert* at the Louvre in Paris on the 2nd of January of that year. He then sent it off to press, and himself proceeded in a vessel, manned by destitute Englishmen in France, to found a new colony for the Queen in Virginia. He set sail from Normandy, but before he left the English Channel his vessel was captured by one of the Parliament cruizers, and Davenant was imprisoned in Cowes Castle, in the Isle of Wight. Meanwhile *Gondibert* was being printed, and its author, who expected to be hanged from day to day, was just in time to append to it a dejected postscript, dated from his island prison, October 22, 1650, in which he said that no second volume of the poem must be expected.

The book issued under these melancholy auspices was really nothing less than a manifesto from the classical school, on the first occasion which it had found to address the public conjointly. Denham took no part in it, for Denham seems to have had a personal dislike to Davenant. But all the rest were there. The author himself, in a very long and interesting preface to Hobbes, discoursed on heroic poetry in general, and his views of the necessity of a revolution in taste. Our verse, he said, had become lax and trivial, and we needed to be recalled to precision and moral vigour. Hobbes's reply, a very graceful critical essay on the same subject, was printed next; and then followed commendatory copies of verses by Waller and by Cowley. Waller's eulogy was expressed in admirable couplets, polished to the highest pitch, as though on so great an occasion he was bound to show how smooth and dignified the new kind of poetical numbers could be. And thus he sums up the matter of his friend's epic :—

> "Man is thy theme, his virtue or his rage
>   Drawn to the life in each elaborate page;

> Mars nor Bellona are not namèd here,
> But such a Gondibert as both might fear.
> Venus had here, and Hebe, been outshined
> By thy bright Bertha and thy Rhodolind;
> Such is thy happy skill and such the odds
> Between thy worthies and the Grecian gods."

Cowley, in a less skilful address, dwells upon the novelty of Davenant's design, and compares his zeal in starting to colonize a new world, with his enthusiasm in founding a new school in poetry[1]. It is plain that to all the group in Paris the publication of *Gondibert* appeared a very important and epoch-making event.

There is one writer of the nineteenth century whose position in poetical history is so analogous to that of Davenant, that when the idea has once occurred to us, we see the parallel in numberless instances. This is Southey, a learned, ingenious, and fertile writer to whom it is with the greatest hesitation, and more for compliment than merit, that we can allow the title of poet. Like Southey,

---

[1] " Sure 'twas this noble boldness of thy muse
    Did thy desire to seek new worlds infuse,
   And ne'er did Heaven so much a voyage bless,
    If thou canst plant but there with like success."

It seems almost incredible that Newcomb the publisher could complacently print these verses when the " voyage " had just come to so premature and so humiliating a close.

Davenant imposed himself upon his own generation by the force of his character, by the abundance of his writings, and by the tact with which he attached himself to that party which was destined to popularity in the immediate future.

As Southey foresaw that Wordsworth and Coleridge, though in 1800 still the objects of ridicule and dislike, would reign over English poetry in 1830, so Davenant had the wit to see that it was Waller and Denham who in twenty years' time would conquer the field from which they had not as yet begun to dislodge their predecessors; and he came over to their camp with equal frankness and adroitness. Like his later analogue he was supported and encouraged by an extraordinary belief in his own powers and merit. When Southey, in 1837, told the public that his "poetical works had obtained a reputation equal to his wishes; and that he had grounds for hoping that it might not be deemed hereafter more than commensurate with their deserts," we might really be reading one of the clumsy sentences in which the author of *Gondibert* blows his own trumpet. Their strenuous self-praise and dignity of demeanour were a great source of strength alike to Southey and to Davenant, and these personal qualities have so far imposed upon the public, even posthumously, that the true judgment has hardly yet been passed on the one or on the other.

From the point of view of literary history, there must always be room found in our memories for Davenant as for Southey. They were singularly interesting figures, they took a very leading part in the intellectual movement of their times, their mental vigour and their desire to excel in verse combined to give them a prominence in current poetry. Moreover, they both contrived to shelter themselves so snugly under the friendship of great men, that to this day criticism shrinks from dragging them forth into the glare of noon. After all these years it still seems something like treason to Wordsworth, to Landor, to our venerable and admired Sir Henry Taylor, to say that Southey was no poet in the true sense. It shows the wonderful force and clearness of the man that we should be so loath to say it. But nothing can be more certain than that it is true, whether it is agreeable to us to say so or not. The vast tree of his poetical works, with its spreading epic branches, its close foliage of tales and ballads, and its parasitical growths of laureate odes and hymns, is dead at the root, and the wind rustles in its dry leaves. It will stand there in the wood, a vast sapless trunk, a mere historic memorial, while every year its sisters of the forest put forth fresh foliage and renew their youth. So stands Davenant in that closer and more fantastic grove of the seventeenth century, one of the largest of the trees in girth and height, but the deadest of them all, with scarcely a cluster of green buds here and there when the sap rises in the woodland.

To understand the vogue of *Gondibert* in the middle of the seventeenth century, we have to remind ourselves of the reception which our grandfathers and grandmothers gave to *Thalaba* and to the *Curse of Kehama*. As in the case of those shapeless Indian epics, so in that of Davenant's long-winded Lombardian heroic, there were not a few critics and lovers of poetry who refused to bow the knee to a poetical Baal so foreign to the imaginative tradition of the race. But to the public at large the one class of epic and the other were equally attractive for the moment. The strenuous didactic tone of morality, the emphatic wish to improve the condition and raise the dignity of poetry, the gorgeous and exotic imagery with which the improbable, and, indeed, uninteresting tales were adorned, impressed the majority of readers, and secured the elder, as the later poet, a large audience, recruited even from the literary class itself. *Gondibert* was widely read, and still more widely praised. No single poem of the like ambition, and sustained at the like pitch, had been printed in England since Phineas Fletcher's *Purple Island,* published nearly twenty years before.

It was widely praised, as I have said, and still more widely discussed. The form in which it was issued, with the polemical prefaces of the author and of Hobbes, and the manifestoes of Waller and Cowley at the head of it, naturally provoked attention. It was at the publication of *Gondibert* that the leaders of the old school first perceived that a phalanx of young writers was marching to attack them, and hence it was over the body of this poem that the thickest of the fight went on, in the long and hopeless battle of the romantic against the classical influence. The allusions to *Gondibert* in contemporary literature are very numerous, and I possess in my own collection two extremely rare pamphlets entirely dedicated to attacks upon it in verse. They take a somewhat important place in the history of the movement. The first, published in 1653, is entitled *Certain Verses written by several of the Author's friends, to be reprinted with the second edition of Gondibert.* The verses are certainly by four several hands; I believe that

I detect Denham, Cleveland, the younger Donne, and Jasper Mayne as the wicked anonymous quartet[1].

Like most satiric fooling, much of the stinging wit has evaporated out of the rhymes; they are tolerably flat now. But plainly they were calculated to hurt the sensitive and conceited Davenant, who is mercilessly chaffed, under the pseudonym of Dafne, about his name, his personal appearance, his misfortunes as a prisoner, his supposed cowardice in battle, and, a little more legitimately, about the tediousness of his poetry. One satirist makes him describe himself:—

> "I am old Davenant
> With my fustian quill,
> Though skill I have not,
> I must be writing still
> On Gondibert ....
> Waller and Cowley,
> 'Tis true, have praised my book,
> But how untruly
> All they that read may look;
> Nor can old Hobbes defend me."

[1] After forming this conjecture, I discovered, in a copy of the 1653 pamphlet in the library of Yale College, Connecticut, a MS. note in writing of the end of the seventeenth century suggesting that the four authors were Denham, the younger Donne, Sir Allen Broderick and William Crofts.

Another undertakes, in triplets that are sometimes smart, to give a comic summary of the famous epic; another parodies the lumbering quatrains, with their affected new coinages, *abstersive, ethnick*, and the like. One bard picks out the following bundle of adjectives, which he says will serve for any substantive under any circumstances, and he arranges them in a rude elegiac couplet:—

"Nice, wise, important, eager, grave, busy, recorded,
Ancient, abstersive, Roman, experienc'd, shy."

A still rarer pamphlet, *The Incomparable Poem Gondibert vindicated from the Wit Combats of Four Esquires* was published in 1655. This is so rare that I do not happen to have met with any copy but the one which I possess. It has far less literary merit than the former, of which it is a deliberate and painstaking imitation. Each piece contained in the first collection is imitated in the second in exactly the same metre. The writer I take to be the curious poetaster Wild, the author of the *Iter Boreale*. The principal interest it possesses, beyond certain biographical allusions into which it is needless to enter now, is the attitude it takes with regard to the classical school. It dwells on the fact that Denham and young Donne have no right to be laughing at Davenant, for that they and he, and Waller and Cowley as well, are all tarred with the same brush[1], and together form a group of pestilent writers who are seeking to overthrow the tradition of the national poetry. To such a spreading plant the seed that Waller sowed had grown by the year 1655.

We must, however, return to *Gondibert*. To give any account of the story is beyond my power, for though I have read it through with more care than I can recommend to any of my own readers, the tenour of the plot has escaped me. I believe that there is a consecutive story, but it has not been vouchsafed to me to unravel its mystery. There is an incomparable Lombard hero, Gondibert; an old king, Aribert; and his renowned daughter, Rhodolind. The virtuous Prince Gondibert meets in combat a Prince Oswald, no less virtuous than he. A certain Laura, when she sees Oswald slain, finds that her blood flies back into her liver, and she dies. The renowned Rhodolind would love Gondibert, and yet would not, and is so long making up her mind that he loves Berthe.

---

[1]   "You think they feign, that is, they lie,
      That speak of *Gondibert* so high;
      If that their verses were much taller,
      Waller hath since out-Gonded Waller,"

that is to say, no doubt, in the pompous rhetoric of his "Panegyric on Oliver Cromwell" in 1653.

There are also "busy Goltho" and "wise Astragon," and "distempered Ulfinere," to discover whose relation to the pre-named characters would puzzle a professional interpreter of conundrums. The poem, in short, is a *fiasco*, as a narrative poem or epic; its only merit consists in its episodes, and in the sententious vigour of single lines. One of the most graceful episodes, and one which does most credit to Davenant's versification, is that of the hunted stag who takes to the water:—

"This frail relief was like short gales of breath
    Which oft at sea a long dead calm prepare;
Or like our curtains drawn at point of death,
    When all our lungs are spent to give us air.

For on the shore the hunters him attend;
    And whilst the chace grew warm as is the day
(Which now from the hot *zenith* does descend)
    He is imbos'd, and weary'd to a bay.

The jewel, Life, he must surrender here;
    Which the world's mistress, Nature, does not give,
But like dropp'd favours suffers us to weare,
    Such as by which pleas'd lovers think they live.

Yet life he so esteems, that he allows
    It all defence his force and rage can make;
And to the *Regian* race such fury shows
    As their last blood some unreveng'd forsake.

But now the Monarch Murderer comes in,
   Destructive man! whom Nature would not arm,
As when in madness mischief is foreseen
   We leave it weaponless for fear of harm.

For she defenceless made him that he might
   Less readily offend; but Art arms all,
From single strife makes us in numbers fight;
   And by such art this royal stag did fall.

Now weeps till grief does even his murd'rers pierce,—
   Grief which so nobly through his anger strove,
That it deserved the dignity of verse,
   And had it words as humanly would move.

Thrice from the ground his vanquished head he rear'd,
   And with last looks his forest-walks did view;
Where sixty summers he had rul'd the herd,
   And where sharp *dittany* now vainly grew,

Whose hoary leaves no more his wounds shall heal;
   For with a sigh (a blast of all his breath)
That viewless thing call'd Life, did from him steal;
   And with their bugle horns they wind his death.

It will be noticed that the stanza in which *Gondibert* is composed is the four-line heroic stanza with alternate rhymes which Gray made so popular by his *Elegy in a Country Churchyard*. The history of this stanza is somewhat interesting. It was first used for a poem of considerable length by Sir John Davies, an Elizabethan who possessed more than any of his fellows the instinct of the classical school. His *Nosce Teipsum*, a long didactic poem full of thought and dignified rhetoric, was admired by reading men all through the eighteenth century. When I had to examine the commonplace-books of Gray, preserved at Pembroke College, Cambridge, I found that he had been a minute student of the *Nosce Teipsum*, and that he had copied many of its sections. *Gondibert* was the next lengthy essay in the same style[1]; Hobbes immediately adopted it for his translation of Homer[2], and this was followed a dozen years later by Dryden's *Annus Mirabilis*. It was not again employed, so far as I remember, all through the Restoration or the Augustan age nor again until, in 1743, the Earl of Chesterfield brought out the posthumous *Love Elegies* of his young cousin Hammond, which were almost entirely couched in these solemn quatrains.

[1] Davenant's attention may possibly have been called to the metre from the fact that Robert Ellice had used it in his prefatory verses to *Albovine* in 1629.

[2] This is how Hobbes opens his *Iliad*:—

"O Goddess, sing what woe the discontent
 Of Thetis' son brought to the Greeks, what souls
Of heroes down to Erebus it sent,
 Leaving their bodies unto dogs and fowls."

It is believed that the printing of Hammond's verses incited Gray to begin his *Churchyard Elegy*, and to make the four-line stanza the basis of most of his harmonies. But it has not been much used since the end of last century, in spite of Gray's success. The fact is that, while it undoubtedly is the most sonorous and dignified measure in English verse, its incapacity for passion, even for the passion of grief, narrows the ground within which it can be employed. Of the three long seventeenth-century poems which I have mentioned as written in it, there is not one that is not too copious and long-winded for a modern reader. Still it is a curious thing that so noble a stanza should be abandoned altogether, and a young poet who should now employ it to embody a series of grave and philosophical ideas would be rewarded by conveying a sense of novelty in form. *Gondibert*, which, to the monotony of this four-line stanza, adds a turgid weight, a plethora of thought and allusion, copied from Lord Brooke, belongs without doubt to the one class of literature which Voltaire said had no right to exist, the tiresome class. And yet there were hundreds of readers in its own age who did not find it dull[1].

---

[1] It even superseded, for the moment, the French romances which were the darling reading of the ladies. A contemporary ballad says,

Davenant's life was crowded with incidents during the months that succeeded the publication of his epic. He was not hanged at Cowes Castle, as he feared that he should be, but he was removed to the Tower of London, which gave him very little solace in his terrors. He was, in fact, delivered over to be tried by a court of high commission, which was almost tantamount to sending him straight to the scaffold. We learn, however, from his friend Aubrey, that two aldermen of York, to whom he had been very kind when they were prisoners, applied on his behalf to a person of influence with Cromwell, and that his life was saved in this way. What makes this legend extremely pleasant and interesting is that tradition confidently declares the person through whose final interposition Davenant's life was given him to have been Milton, and adds that the Royalist writer recollected this at the Restoration, and pleaded successfully for the safety of the great Puritan. This is one of those stories which are so charming in themselves,

addressing Gondibert:—

>"Thou art the public *Icon morum*,
> The ladies lay the book before 'em,
> And *Polexander's* not o' the quorum.
>
> Before they treat a Lord, a part
> Of thee is read or got by heart;
> They're catechised in *Gondibert*."

and so flattering to the better instincts of human nature, that we do not desire to pry too minutely into the evidence upon which they are based. Davenant languished in the Tower of London for two years, and then was allowed quietly to emerge and live at peace.

A final impetus was given by Davenant to the classical manner in poetry in his attempts to amuse the fashionables with dramatic pastimes before the Restoration came about. The operas and rhymed tragedies cast a pale shadow before them in the shape of *The Entertainment at Rutland House* in 1656. This was a very dreary and timid succession of soliloquies in prose[1], with, however, a prologue and an epilogue in the heroic couplet, neither of which show any great aptitude for distich. But in September of the same year Davenant printed the long opera of *The Siege of Rhodes*, quite a volume in itself, most of the recitative of which is written in heroic couplet. The best of it has by this time become so like Waller's verse as to be undistinguishable from it. The following passage from *The Siege of Rhodes* is typical of the rest, and contains no single tone or ring of the versification

---

[1] The *Entertainment* is really a polemical treatise, in dialogue form, on behalf of the drama. It is difficult to know what Davenant meant by styling it an "opera."

which Davenant used during his youth or middle age:—

"Pale show those crescents to our bloody cross;
Sink not the western kingdoms in our loss?
Will not the Austrian eagle moult her wings,
That long have hovered o'er the Gallic kings?
Whose lilies too will wither when we fade,
And the English lion sink into a shade.
Thou see'st not, whilst so young and guiltless too,
That Kings mean seldom what their statesmen do;
Who measure not the compass of a crown
To fit the head that wears it, but their own;
Still hindering peace, because they stewards are,
Without account, to that wild spender, war."

This verse, as I have said, might just as well be Waller's as Davenant's. The note of individuality is removed from it. And this leads me to speak of one strange and distressing characteristic of the classical school in poetry, its horror of the personal, the individual accent. Among the romantic poets of every age, the great aim has been the expression of personal conviction, of personal experience. We know the great poets by their phrases. For instance, who but Spenser would have written:—

"So fair and fresh that Lady showed herself in sight;"

who but Shakespeare :—

"Rough winds do shake the darling buds of May;"
and who but Milton :—

"Busiris and his Memphian chivalry"?

These instances I give at random, the memory of each of my readers will recall others at least as cogent. From each of these it is not too fanciful to say that we could build up some sort of theory of the poetic character of the man, and catch an intuition of Spenser's long-drawn, perfumed sweetness, of the versatility and manly tenderness of Shakespeare, of Milton's voluble grandeur. But it would not be possible, or at least if it be possible it is so because the character of a great man *will* assert itself, to detect this individuality in any single line of the classical poets from Waller to Darwin. With them the effort was towards a composite thing, a vehicle to be used by all scholars who were also artists in verse, and this thing which they combined to polish and to refine was the iambic distich. The poet was no longer Teucer, forging his own yew-tree shafts, and sending them whither he would, but merely one member of a regiment of archers, always sharpening their burning arrows, but acting in concert, and in obedience to certain set rules of warfare.

I proposed, however, at the outset of this chapter, to devote it to Cowley as well as to Davenant; and already three-fourths of my space has been given to the latter. I am the less concerned at this, partly because I have already, in my volume of *Seventeenth Century Studies*, given a very minute examination to the life and writings of Cowley, and partly because the position he holds in the history of the classical movement is much less influential than that of Davenant. He was, no doubt, a poet of a far higher class than Davenant, the only poet, indeed, of very high native merit between the romantic school and Dryden, but his allegiance to the classical innovators was only half-hearted. He was their friend and companion, he was associated with them in political ambition and in the adversity of exile, and he was too vivid, too modern, not to be interested by what they were doing and to be affected by it. But while Waller, Denham, Davenant, and, by-and-by, such followers as Lower, Katharine Philips, and Lord Orrery, fade into one entity, and are, as we have seen, almost undistinguishable, Cowley was much too strong to relinquish his individuality even for the sake of endowing his country with a school of correct writers.

Cowley, like Davenant, had begun to write among the romantic poets. He was a precocious Cambridge verseman, the author of three successful volumes of poetry before he ceased to be an undergraduate, and the influences of the university clung to him strongly through life. What those influences were in the second quarter of the seventeenth century we may see in such highly-coloured, elaborate, and hyper-intellectual poems as the *Psyche* of Joseph Beaumont and the *Psychozoia* of Henry More, distinguished members of the university during Cowley's undergraduate days. There was an attempt made at Cambridge to sanctify the rainbow fancies of the Marinist school by hallowing them to sacred uses. Crashaw did this in one way, and Milton, in his *Nativity Ode*, in another,—the thing was a Cambridge fashion[1]. They were very pious, all these youths, very earnest, glowing and ingenious, and their work has been too hastily confounded with that of the cavalier song-writers and courtier forgers of concetti.

From this interesting school of Cambridge

---

[1]   " Meanwhile the rural ditties were not mute,
      Temper'd to th' oaten flute."

See, also, the lines in which Dr Lany, Master of Pembroke, is congratulated by Crashaw on being surrounded by "a Pierian flock" of pious young poets, in 1631.

writers, Cowley emerged, the last and the most exhausted of them all. It seemed as if all the azure and the scarlet and the amber had been squandered before he appeared; and his conceits,—if it be not too much of a conceit to say so,—look as if they had been drawn, but never filled up in colour. With him, rhetoric takes the place of a coloured fancy, and the development of rhetoric in his verse was what drew him towards Waller, whose work was all in the direction of oratorical effect. I am inclined to think that Cowley was born with gifts in the way of poetic rhetoric which have scarcely been excelled. He is so extremely unequal that he almost eludes criticism, but at his very best he possesses, more perhaps than any other English writer, that peculiar Latin magnificence of phrase which is so characteristic of Victor Hugo. I am ready to withdraw the suggestion the moment that I have made it, so absurd does it seem to compare the author of *Les Châtiments* with the author of *Davideis*. But if I am distinctly understood to mean no more than this, that in the rare passages where Cowley excels, it is with a tendency towards the excellence so general in Victor Hugo, I wish to retain the criticism. To my ear, the close of the elegy on Cowley, which I will now read, has this quality of Hugo; the passage is, moreover, valuable in our present inquiry as showing to how great an extent Cowley, when he chose, and as early as 1650, conformed to Waller's new rules for the conduct of the heroic couplet :—

"Pardon, my *Mother Church*[1], if I consent,
That *angels* led him when from thee he went;
For even in *error* sure no *danger* is
When join'd with so much *piety* as *his*.
Ah, mighty *God*, with shame I speak't, and grief,
Ah that our greatest *faults* were in *belief!*
And our weak *reason* were ev'n weaker yet,
Rather than thus our *wills* too strong for it.
His *faith* perhaps in some nice tenets might
Be wrong; his *life*, I'm sure, was *in the right*.
And I myself a *Catholic* will be,
So far, at least, great *Saint*, to *pray* to thee.
Hail, *Bard triumphant!* and some care bestow
On *us*, the *Poets Militant* below!
Oppos'd by our old enemy, adverse *Chance*,
Attack'd by *Envy*, and by *Ignorance*,
Enchain'd by *Beauty*, tortur'd by *Desires*,
Expos'd by *Tyrant-Love* to savage *beasts* and *fires*.
Thou from low earth in nobler *flames* didst rise,
And like *Elijah*, mount alive the skies,

---

[1] I leave the italics as Cowley printed them, for I believe that they represent his own view of the points where stress and emphasis should be laid by the reader.

Elisha-like (but with a wish much less.
More fit thy *greatness*, and my *littleness*)
Lo here I beg, (I whom thou once didst prove
So humble to *esteem*, so good to love),
Not that thy *spirit* might on me *doubled* be,
I ask but half thy mighty *spirit* for me,
And when my *Muse* soars with so strong a wing,
'Twill learn of things *divine*, and first of *Thee* to sing."

This is very tender and beautiful, I think; quite an oasis of real literature to cheer us in our journey through the wilderness. But the individuality of Cowley is too strong in this to make it a good example of classical writing. The principal contribution which he made to the new order of style was a sacred epic, on the history of David, which I suspect of being as little read in the present day as any epic poem in existence. It does not, to be frank, invite perusal, although it would not be Cowley's if it did not contain a great many oddities and a certain number of beauties. Its principal interest is that it is the earliest example of a sustained narrative poem in the new distich, and it is quite plain that if Cowley had only possessed a little more genius and Milton a little less, there would have been the greatest possible chance that the couplet would have become the normal epic form with us, as it had become with the French. Fortunately Milton showed us a better way. We may recollect any passage of *Paradise Regained*, and compare it with the following fragment from Cowley's *Davideis*.

"Whilst thus his wrath with threats the *tyrant* fed,
The threatned *youth* slept fearless on his bed;
Sleep on, rest quiet as thy *conscience* take,
For though *thou* sleep'st thy self, thy *God's* awake!
Above the subtle foldings of the sky,
Above the well-set *orbs'* soft *harmony*,
Above those petty *lamps* that gild the *night*,
There is a place o'erflown with hallowed *light*,
Where *Heaven*, as if it left it self behind,
Is stretcht out far, nor its own bounds can find:
Here *peaceful flames* swell up the sacred place,
Nor can contain themselves in th' endless space.
For there no twilight of the *sun's* dull ray,
Glimmers upon the pure and native day;
No pale-fac'd *moon* does in stol'n beams appear,
Or with dim *taper* scatters *darkness* there;
On no smooth *sphere* the restless *seasons* slide,
No circling *motion* doth swift *time* divide;
Nothing is there *To come*, and nothing *Past*,
But an *eternal Now* does always last.
There sits th' *Almighty*, *First* of all, and *End*,
Whom nothing but *Himself* can comprehend;
Who with his *word* commanded *all* to *be*,
And *all* obey'd him, for that *word* was *He*.

While examining Cowley's position in the poetic literature of the age, we are struck by the fact that he was with the classicists, yet not of them. Their relations were with antiquity through France, his with antiquity through Spain. I am not certain that I perceive in his writings any direct imitation of Spanish literature, but he has the *cultismo*, the desire to speak politely and artificially, which the critics of the age rightly identified with the poets of Madrid. His great influence, his great prestige, clashed with those of Waller, and after having at least as much to do with forming Dryden's style as Waller had, Cowley sank into the second rank. Pope, while bending respectfully to Waller and Denham, could sneer at Cowley[1], and treat him as a dethroned monarch of literature.

But a curious thing happened. When the prestige of Pope himself was waning at last, and when Waller began to fade back into disrepute, the prosody of Cowley revived once more, and in the hands of Gray became the main poetic in-

---

[1] Who now reads Cowley? If he pleases yet
His Moral pleases, not his pointed wit;
Forgot his epic, nay Pindaric art,
But still I love the language of his heart.

Pope: *Imitations of Horace*. Bk. ii. Epis. 1. 1741.

fluence of the middle of the eighteenth century. It was the echo of Cowley's harmonies that broke the monotonous twanging of the distich, and in Shelley, in Coleridge, in the fluent and ingenious inventions of Mr Swinburne, we still hear variations upon that broken lyrical music, while the brilliant couplet that Waller was so assiduous in introducing has quite passed away out of our living literature.

THE REACTION.

THE REACTION.

THE student who considers the luxuriance of English lyrical and descriptive poetry in the early part of the seventeenth century finds himself easily amazed at the suddenness of the decline into the prosaic school. The enclosure of British verse, soon after the death of Shakespeare, was less like a rich and crowded garden of the usual sort than like the famous parterre of "Mistress Mary, all contrary," in which, as we know, there were "silver bells and cockle-shells and pretty maids all of a row." It was a mixture, as mad as any which the human mind is able to conceive, of real ornament and fictitious, the fresh rose-bud and the painted rose and the mock-rose made of pink paper, all planted and blowing side by side. Now throughout the history of the world it is to be noted that literature of this sort,—to which we give the general title of Alexandrian, because in the eclipse of Greece it flourished at Alexandria,—needs but a breath to disappear. When it is most gay and floribund, it is so close to the borders of dissolution, that the passage of a cloud over its surface, a change in the direction of the wind, is sufficient to destroy it. Its prosperity is only partially real. It contains the elements of beauty, fragrance, brightness, but the absence of literary sincerity is fatal to its permanence. I speak here of this sort of hybrid literature in general, whether we meet with it in Egypt or in Spain, in the France of the Pléiade or in the England of the disciples of Donne; but in the latter instance everything conspired to make the process of decay particularly irresistible and complete.

Hence we have hitherto noted no opposition to the new forms of poetical writing. So far as we have yet proceeded it was indeed quite inconsiderable. Waller put out his discovery, his fascinating new form, and the young poets only needed to perceive it, to understand what he was talking about, to follow him like sheep[1]. He piped his

---

[1]   "Such tributes are, like tenures, only fit
To show from whom we hold our right to wit,"

says Aphara Behn, in reference to the imitations of Waller which were becoming universal. In another place, absolutely intoxicated with the new form of writing, she declares, addressing Waller:—

"Long did the untuned world in ignorance stray,
Producing nothing that was great or gay,
Till taught by thee the true poetic way."

shrill monotonous treble, like the man of Hamelin, and the streets of the Marinists were emptied. It has, at all events, up to this moment seemed desirable to represent him as doing this. His heterodoxy so rapidly and so smoothly became orthodoxy that it appeared to be most accurate to give an impression of the movement, as of a stream, which, once having filtered through the dam, simply gains in volume as it proceeds, and presently carries all before it.

Yet as a matter of fact, to pursue our simile, a good deal of water remained for a long time in the old channel, and some spurted with vehemence in an independent direction, and tried to create a new diversion for itself. It is time that we should pause and consider these two classes of reaction, active and passive, neither of which was capable of doing more than diversify the history of the period, since neither can be said to have delayed the triumph of the classical forms by a single day. First, then, we may discuss the recusants who saw that a change in the style of English poetry was needed, but who were not content to make that change in the mode which Waller and Denham indicated. The aim of these writers was to restore poetry to a rugged English force, to dismiss the elegancies of a Gallic style, and to strengthen verse without abandoning the overflow.

The aim so laid down, more or less consciously, by Cleveland first and then by Wild, was one with which it is possible for a modern critic to sympathize. It was, in fact, an admirable notion born out of due time, and one which, if it could have been carried out, might have obviated all succeeding revolutions in poetic taste. A strong romantic poetry, freed from the tawdry ornament of the Marinists, was a middle course between Donne and Waller, which it would have been a happy thing if Cleveland could have seen his way to create. But the instinct of the people was against it in the middle of the seventeenth century. There was a craving after elegance, directness, lucidity, and to secure these qualities the public was prepared to surrender everything else without a sigh.

Neither Cleveland nor Wild has contrived to keep a place for himself in the history of English literature. I do not know any book on poetry, however detailed, which gives even the slightest notice of the latter. Cleveland has succeeded, chiefly on the tradition that he pointed the way to *Hudibras*, in keeping a very shadowy hold upon students. But from the historian of style he claims a great deal more than this. A bitter and determined foe to Marinism in his mature years, he began life as a Marinist of the most frantic species. The rage for ingenious similes, for twisted images of the fancy, was perhaps never carried to so monstrous an excess in any language as it is in Cleveland's scarcely intelligible love-poems, the *Senses' Festival* and the *Fuscara*[1]. Having sown his poetical wild oats in this way, at Cambridge, where, we are told, his verses were voted too extravagant even at that sanctum and high altar of extravagance, he turned satirist, and as a waspish cavalier in the train of Charles, he did his best to madden the roundheads with rough metrical

---

[1] Thus, in *Fuscara*, he plays upon the notion that a bee has been settling on his mistress's hand:—

"He perches now upon her wrist,
A proper hawk for such a fist,
Making that flesh his bill of fare,
Which hungry cannibals would spare,
Where lilies in a lovely brown
Inoculate carnation;"

(that is to say, the wrist is freckled)

"He[r] *argent* skin with *or* so streamed
As if the milky way were creamed,"

(by her small, invisible golden hairs);

"From hence he to the wood-bine bends
That quivers at her finger-ends,
That run division on the tree
Like a thick-branching pedigree,"

and so on.

tirades, until, in 1655, he was seized at Norwich, and crushed, as a wasp is crushed.

Cleveland betrays a curious sense of his own failure as a poet; he is on the borderland of distinction, but he never quite crosses it. He would fain have made his gift of real service to the State, as young fellows to this day protest about "the might of poesy." But he was conscious all the time that he was not a force. He says:—

"O that I could but vote myself a poet!
Or had the legislative knack to do it!
Or like the doctors militant, could get
Dubbed at adventurers' Verser Bannaret[1]!"

When we see him cheering Prince Rupert on to slaughter, or rating the rebel Scots like a fish-wife, or pouring out a soldierly extravagance of grief in *Charles' Spikenard*, we think of the siege of Newark, the desperate flight from Norwich, and we sigh to think of the misfortunes of the King's too-eager Verser Bannaret.

Cleveland was a disappointment in politics, in sword-craft, and even in poetry. But he had an inkling of several remarkable things. Not only did he lead the way for *Hudibras*, about which much might be said if we were here considering the history of humoristic literature in England, but

[1] *Rupertismus*, 1—4.

he saw various truths with regard to metre and rhythm which had not been perceived by any writer before him. One of the chief of these was the great variety of cadence which was possible in English verse. Up to his time and to that of Waller, the triple or anapæstic cadence, which is now so familiar to us, and which the facilities of its use have even vulgarized, had not been used since the pre-Chaucerian epoch. The great Elizabethan poets had achieved their marvellous effects without its ever occurring to them that they had at their elbow a dancing or lilting cadence which the very ballads of the peasantry might have revealed to them. It is in fact exactly when they abandoned themselves to the loose ballad-rhythms that they approached it nearest. Shakespeare, of course, in such songs as "Come away, come away, Death!" glides into the triple cadence, and so, as Mr Coventry Patmore points out, does the early Elizabethan Phaer, in his version of the *Æneid*. I have remarked another instance in a ballad of Bishop Corbet's. But these felicities were the result either of accident, or, in the case of Shakespeare, for instance, of an art above artifice. There are but few instances of the deliberate use of English dactyls or anapæsts until the period we are examining.

It would be a very remarkable thing if we should discover that we owe not merely our serried couplet without overflow, but our dancing and tripping cadence also to Waller. It would point him out to us as one of the most vivid metrical inventors in our literature; and I do not think we can deny him this second glory in addition to the first. In his 1645 volume of *Poems* there is a copy of verses called *Chloris and Hilas*, which is written in faltering, but unmistakable dactyls. Waller long afterwards said that it was composed to imitate the motion of a saraband. Here are certain portions of it, those in which the triple cadence is most audible:—

> "Hilas, O Hilas, why sit we mute,
>   Now that each bird saluteth the Spring;
> Wind up the slackenèd strings of thy lute,
>   Never can'st thou want matter to sing!
>   *   *   *   *   *   *   *
> Sweetest, you know, the sweetest of things
>   Of various flowers the bees do compose,
> Yet no particular taste it brings
>   Of violet, woodbine, pink or rose."

These stanzas, as our ear will instruct us, are built up on three beats and a pause,

"Wind up the | slackenèd | strings of thy | lute"

exactly on the plan, though not with the agility and skill, of the cadences in Moore's *Lalla Rookh*:—

"Who has not | heard of the | vale of Cash | mere?"

And this was a discovery, which, if we may attribute it to Waller, raises him to the dignity of a poetical Columbus. But this is in itself a dubious and apparently accidental thing; Waller attained it almost by chance, through his surprising quickness of ear in imitation, but he does not seem to have known what he had found, nor to have tried to repeat his experiment. Cleveland, on the other hand, deliberately studied, not once, but repeatedly, dactylic effects of a really very delicate kind. The first edition of Cleveland's *Poems* was published in 1647; but on this we can build no theory of Waller's priority of composition. Born eight years earlier than Cleveland, Waller is likely to have been first in the field. But as Cleveland's lyrical poems are, I believe, practically unknown even to scholars, and as this point of the introduction of the triple cadence is one of the greatest interest, I will quote one or two examples. In a strange, half-mad, indecorous lyric called *Mark Anthony*, I find these lines:—

"When as the nightingale chanted her vespers,
  And the wild forester crouched on the ground,

> Venus invited me in th' evening whispers
> Unto a fragrant field with roses crowned."

This drags a little; but the intention is incontestable. This is better:—

> "Mystical grammar of amorous glances,
> Feeling of pulses, the physic of love,
> Rhetorical courtings, and musical dances,
> Numb'ring of kisses arithmetic prove."

Another poem, called *Square-Cap*, evidently written at Cambridge in the author's undergraduate days, gives us a totally distinct variety of the anapæstic cadence:—

> "Come hither Apollo's bouncing girl,
> And in a whole Hippocrene of Sherry,
> Let's drink a round till our brains do whirl,
> Tuning our pipes to make ourselves merry;
> A Cambridge lass, Venus-like, born of the froth
> Of an old half-filled jug of barley-broth,
> She, she is my mistress, her suitors are many,
> But she'll have a square-cap, if e'er she have any."

There is quite a ring of John Byrom or of Shenstone in these last lines, the precursors of so much that has pleased the ears of the eighteenth and nineteenth centuries[1].

---

[1] The cantering measure, in its prettiest form, however, first appears in our literature in one of the "terrestrial hymns and carnal

The Reaction. 191

I have permitted myself to dwell a little on these characteristics of Cleveland, although the great movement which we are considering swept by him. It swept still more impetuously past another man, who, being born a generation later, attempted to move the body of English poetry when it had gained a still greater impetus in the classical direction. Of Dr Robert Wild, author of the *Iter Boreale*, extremely little is known. He was a Nonconformist divine, and a free lance in politics, ready to attack either side on a slight provocation. Although in the nature of his talent he closely resembled Cleveland, they were at the extreme ends of opposite camps, and Wild's chief occupation was the defence of the Presbyterians, as it was Cleveland's chief delight to attack them.

ejaculations" of Alexander Radcliffe, a very clever but most disreputable literary soldier of the Restoration. One of his songs, in *The Ramble*, 1682, runs thus:—

> "Away with these fellows' contriving,
>   They've spoilt all our pleasant design,
> We were once in a way of true living,
>   Improving discourse with good wine;
> But now conversation grows tedious,
>   Over coffee they still confer notes,
> 'Stead of authors both learn'd and facetious,
>   They quote only Dugdale and Oates."

This sounds like a far away premonition of Praed.

Indeed, it seems to have been a couplet of Cleveland's:—

"Had Cain been Scot God would have changed his doom,
  Not forc'd him wander, but confin'd him home[1],"

which aroused the indignation that brought forth Wild's most successful verses, the *Iter Boreale*. During the anarchical protectorate of Richard Cromwell, Wild was certainly the most popular living English poet. His verse, full of local and momentary allusions, was inspired by the rage and doubt that occupied men's minds, and when at last he celebrated the winter journey of General Monk in 1659 in a long poem, which was really a manifesto against Lambert and the Cabal, his popularity among the party now in the ascendant was overwhelming.

The *Iter Boreale* is a deliberate attempt, as I read it, to foist Monk[2] upon the English nation as a successor to Oliver Cromwell, perhaps as a successor to Charles I., with a happy side-

---

[1] From *The Rebel Scot*. The influence of this and other satires of Cleveland upon the style of Dryden deserves close attention. "Lord! what a godly thing is want of shirts!" is an example of pure pre-Drydenic Dryden. But Marvel was Cleveland's most direct pupil in satire.

[2] "MONK! the great *Monk!* that syllable outshines
  Plantagenet's bright name, or *Constantine's*."
  Iter Boreale, ii. 21, 22.

suggestion that if this is not welcome to the public,

"We have another Charles to fetch from Spain."

Wild, in this boisterous and vigorous poem, shows himself the immediate harbinger of the Restoration. The pieces by which during ten years past he had won the favour of the public have, some of them, a more genuine poetical merit. His writing is mostly in heroic couplets, of the kind Cleveland had used, less straggling and licentious in form than the old verse, but full of abbreviations and rude transpositions of accent[1]. He was not ignorant of the great changes which were being introduced into English prosody, nor did he wholly reject them. He does not, so far as I remember, mention any poets of the romantic school; but he speaks of Denham, Cowley, and Davenant in terms of surly respect, and acknowledges their poetic supremacy, even while he satirizes them, while for Waller,—

---

[1] These peculiarities are easily exemplified. For instance:

"Yet, yet he liv'd, stout heart, he liv'd to be
  Depriv'd, driv'n out, and kept out, liv'd to see
  Wars, blazing stars, torches, which Heaven nev'r burns
  But to light kings or kingdoms to their urns."

              Wild: On the Death of Mr Calamy.

"great poet and true prophet too"—he reserves an enthusiasm which is not common to his nature.

By far the most pleasing of Wild's pieces, however, is a lyrical record of his early failure in life, his education at Cambridge serving only, in the absence of patronage and preferment, to accentuate the miseries of enforced idleness and poverty. It is a curious picture of life under the Commonwealth, and it is written in a romantic and singular measure[1], with great earnestness of feeling; among the literature of the age I know nothing that quite resembles it:—

> "In a melancholy study,
>   None but myself,
> Methought my Muse grew muddy;
>   After seven years' reading,
>   And costly breeding,
> I felt, but could find no pelf;
> Into learnèd rags
>   I've rent my plush and satin,
> And now am fit to beg
>   In Hebrew, Greek and Latin;
> Instead of Aristotle,
>   Would I had got a patten.
> Alas! poor scholar! whither wilt thou go?

[1] Imitated twenty years afterwards by Cleland in his ingenious lyric *Hallo my fancy*.

The Reaction.

    Cambridge, now I must leave thee,
        And follow fate,
    College hopes do deceive me;
            I oft expected
            To have been elected,
      But desert is reprobate.
    Masters of colleges
        Have no common graces,
    And they that have fellowships
        Have but commonplaces,
    And those that scholars are
        Must have handsome faces:
Alas! poor scholar! whither wilt thou go?

    I have bow'd, I have bendèd,
        And all in hope
    One day to be befriended:
            I have preached, I have printed
            Whate'er I hinted
      To please our English Pope;
    I worship't towards the East,
        But the Sun doth now forsake me;
    I find that I am falling,
        The Northern winds do shake me:
    Would I had been upright
        For bowing now will break me;
Alas! poor scholar! whither wilt thou go?

Into some country Village
  Now I must go,
Where neither tithe nor tillage
    The greedy patron
    And parchèd matron
  Swear to the Church they owe:
Yet if I can preach
  And pray too on a sudden,
And confute the Pope
  At adventure, without studying,
Then—ten pounds a year,—
  Besides a Sunday pudden.
Alas! poor scholar! whither wilt thou go?

Ships, ships, ships I discover,
  Crossing the main;
Shall I go in, and go over,
    Turn Jew or Atheist,
    Turk or Papist,
  To Geneva or Amsterdam?
Bishoprics are void
  In Scotland,—shall I thither?
Or follow Windebank
  And Finch, to see if either
Do want a priest to shrive them?
  O no! 'tis blustering weather.
Alas! poor scholar! whither wilt thou go?"

At last he decides that nothing is left for him but to be a schoolmaster, and he makes up his mind to spend all his talents and acquirements in the beggarly task of scourging a little Latin into a parcel of thankless urchins.

The same year, 1659, that saw the publication of the *Iter Boreale,* saw that of the first production of a poet who stands alone among the writers of his time, and who must now occupy our attention. William Chamberlayne was born in 1619, fourteen years after the birth of Waller, at Shaftesbury, in Dorsetshire. He lived in that town for seventy years, until in January, 1689, he died there, and was buried in the churchyard by a son to whom he had given the sounding and romantic name of Valentine Chamberlayne. If any of my readers happen to know the town of Shaftesbury, they will easily understand why I compare it to the career of its poet, and find in it a fit emblem of Chamberlayne's position. Shaftesbury stands on the crown of an abrupt hill of greensand, looking over the Vale of Blackmore, between two pastoral rivers not unknown to song, the Stour and the Nadder; its churchyard, where Chamberlayne lies buried, looks out from the terrace of this mimic fastness, the isolation of which may be gathered from the fact that, to this day, no railway has attempted to approach its outposts. What Shaftesbury is among the gentle and accessible market-towns of Dorsetshire, that Chamberlayne was among the poets of the Commonwealth. He was separated, not merely from the new classical school, but from the old Marinist school. He is not a Marinist at all; he goes back much farther for his inspiration, he inherits much from Browne, much from Sidney, much from the followers of Spenser.

Chamberlayne, as we have said, lived all his life at Shaftesbury, where he was a physician. Some of his best years seem to have been spent, at the intervals of his professional work, in writing his great heroic poem of *Pharonnida*, which is one of the longest works in verse in the English language, extending to 13,000 lines, or very considerably more than *Paradise Lost*. In addition to this epic, he wrote a very pretty tragi-comedy, called *Love's Victory*, in which the swains talk West Country dialect, just as they do to the present day. We only know of a single occasion upon which Chamberlayne strayed from his native precincts. He happened to be closing the second book of his *Pharonnida* in the autumn of 1644, when he put down the poem, as he quaintly tells his readers, to fight in a battle for the King. He promises that

> "if in
> This rising storm of blood, which doth begin
> To drop already, I'm not washed into
> The grave, my next safe quarter shall renew
> Acquaintance with *Pharonnida*. Till then,
> I leave the Muses, to converse with men."

He conversed with the men of the Parliament at the indecisive battle of Newbury, on the 27th of October, and, happily for us, returned safe and sound to Shaftesbury to take up the history of the fair Pharonnida where he laid it down.

In the first of these chapters, in order to give a typical and even an extreme example of romantic versification, I quoted an early passage from Keats. Almost any page from Chamberlayne would have served my purpose equally well, but in this connection it is extremely interesting to note the relation of Keats to the Cavalier doctor. Quite lately, it has been pointed out that a very peculiar phrase is transferred bodily into *Endymion* from the *Pharonnida*, and now that Keats' knowledge of Chamberlayne is proved we can only wonder that none of us ever observed before how much *Endymion* owes to the elder and less-known poem. The versification is exactly of the same order; Chamberlayne leaps from rhyme to rhyme, treating them like mere stepping-stones in the stream of his song, exactly as Keats does, and Campbell's simile that the heroic couplet wandered at its own free will through a wilderness of sweets, is equally applicable to the one poet or to the other. This characteristic, of course, gives Chamberlayne a unique position among the writers of his time, all the rest of whom, even if they had not absolutely followed Waller into the enclosure of the distich, were agreed that verse had to mend its ways, and take a measured and decorous step.

The story of *Pharonnida* is laid in modern Greece, the Greece of the poet's day, and from this circumstance its episodes occasionally give us a faint but curious foretaste of the romances of Byron and Anastatius Hope. The rage against the Turk is curious, and it should be interesting to modern Greeks to note that at a date when the Cretan poet Chortakes was almost the sole Hellenic writer who was trying to keep the flame of Greek patriotism alight, an English physician in a little Dorsetshire borough was occupying himself in romantic dreams of Epirote liberty. Campbell, who was pleased to be the first critic to resuscitate the *Pharonnida*, styles it "one of the most interesting stories that ever was told in verse." I cannot go with him so far, although a good many years ago I contrived to read it right through with no excessive weariness. The versification produces a curious feeling in the reader as he proceeds; the student of *Endymion* may have felt the same. It is something like what every one of us may have noticed in the movement of a startled snake in a meadow. Now it flies, long drawn out, over the dry tops of the grasses, now it sinks and seems to writhe into a knot at the bases of the stalks, now it mounts and coils again, now bounds in a glittering quivering line under the open sky. The progress of the reptile is continuous, and ultimately in one visible direction, but its deviations are excessive, and in its less strenuous moments it goes over ten times the ground that is needful for the purpose of its progress. Already accustomed in these chapters to the regular alternate movement of the classical verse, the uniform tramp of the distich, I think my readers will feel a strong contrast in the curious serpentine movement of Chamberlayne's verse in the *Pharonnida*. Here is the passage in which the hero, Argalia, wins his freedom through the violent deaths of the Turk, Ammurat, and his mistress, Janusa :—

"And here the speed Death's messengers did make
 To hurry forth their souls, did faintly shake

Her words into imperfect accents. This,
She cries, is our last interview—a kiss
Then joins their bloodless lips—each close the eyes
Of the other, whilst the parting spirit flies
Mounted on both their breaths, the latest gasp
They ere must draw. Whilst with stiff arms they clasp
Each other's neck, Argalia through a cloud
Of liquid sorrow did behold the proud
Triumphs of death in their untimely fate;
He sees great Ammurat for a robe of state
Grovelling in blood, the fair Janusa lie,
Purpled in death, like polished ivory
Dipped in vermilion; the bright crystals, that
Her soul in conquering flames looked thorough at,
Both quenched and cooled in death. But time did lend
His tears scarce passage, till a drop could end
Its journey o'er his cheeks, before a page,
Whose cruelty had far out-grown his age,
Enters in haste; and with an anger that,
Though indiscreet, his wrongs seems kindled at,
In wounds did on the bassa's body vent
A spleen that death's discharge could not content."

Chamberlayne was altogether too remote as a country practitioner to attract any notice, or to exercise any influence. He had no acquaintances among the literary class; as he says, "Fortune hath placed me in too low a sphere to be happy in the acquaintance of the age's more celebrated wits."

Had he possessed thrice the genius that he had, he must have remained obscure to his own contemporaries. His opposition, therefore, to the classical movement was passive and accidental. The same cannot be said of that of Thomas Stanley, the next name that meets us in the list of the little band who resisted the new forms and the applications of Waller. In 1649, in the middle of the Commonwealth, there appeared a very small volume of poems[1], now extremely rare, which should have prepared readers for a poet of quite a different order from what was then in the ascendant. It was a little collection of idyllic pieces from the latest Greek and Latin writers, the *Europa* of Moschus, the *Cupido Cruci affixus* of Ausonius, the *Pervigilium Veneris* of an unknown but probably African poet. Now, if it be true that we may know a man by the company he keeps, it is no less true that we may know a person of letters by the books that he likes. Thomas Stanley, who was then a young man of four-and-twenty, revealed his taste beyond all manner of doubt when he chose Moschus and Ausonius from all the Greek and Roman curriculum to be the darlings of his Muse.

[1] "Europa. Cupid Crucified. Venus Vigils. With annotations. By Tho. Stanley Esq. London. Printed by W. W. for Humphrey Moseley. 1649."

We shall presently find how characteristic of the man was such a choice. In the meantime, let us see who and what he himself was.

Stanley was born, it appears, in 1625, so that he was by twenty years Waller's junior. He came up to Cambridge, and was entered as a gentleman-commoner at Pembroke, a foundation which, for its size and wealth, has produced or nourished a greater proportion of the English poets than any other educational body in the nation. His tutor was, moreover, the son of the famous Edward Fairfax, the incomparable translator of Tasso, himself a nimble versifier, who was likely to impress on an eager pupil the traditions of a great literary house. Stanley was neither poor nor a recluse; an offshoot of the family of the Earls of Derby, he was aristocratically reared and wealthily supported. He left Cambridge, not, as Wild did, to starve upon his five wits in a village school, but to spend some years in making the grand tour, and in gaining that learned and literary acquaintance with the modern languages of Europe for which he became distinguished. Anthony à Wood says that he possessed one fair estate, and that he married a wife who brought to him another. He was a gentleman of generous fortune and ample leisure. All this is reflected in his poetry, but all this, in combination with his political bias, which was strongly royalist, makes it the more observable that he was absolutely unaffected by the new school. Chamberlayne, in his Dorsetshire fastness, might know nothing of what Waller and Denham and Davenant were doing, but a man of leisure and fashion, like Stanley, could not be so ignorant. The position he took must have been deliberate, and consequent upon the irresistible tenour of his taste.

When a young fellow prefers Moschus to Homer, and Ausonius to Virgil, we know how to class him. We accuse him of a little affectation, of a great love of what is flowery, rococo, and even morbid, and of a certain persistent preference for what the world has decided to reject as sickly and over-ripe. In our days we have witnessed an alarming recrudescence of this sort of taste. It has been fostered by certain developments of the fine arts, it has found itself a voice in certain schools of criticism. I am far from wishing to insinuate that such schools and such developments are wanting in intelligence, or that they do not reply to genuine demands from the modern spirit. But I hold that they are dangerous, because Alexandrian and sickly. The hues on the dying dolphin are exquisite, no doubt, but it will soon be a dead dolphin, and a very disgusting object of study. In the age of the

Commonwealth culture was less broad than it now is, though perhaps it was deeper. At all events, it was not easy, without quite unusual scholarship, to stray so far afield as to strike upon Ausonius and Moschus.

Stanley, as we have said, was a very fine scholar, and his instinct led him to the authors who had possessed in antiquity the romantic and somewhat morbid colouring that he desired. His *Cupid Crucified* is perhaps the prettiest as it certainly seems to be the most faithful piece of translated work done in that age. Ausonius' original is excessively pretty, and Stanley loses very little in putting the soft hexameters into English. The whole is exactly like a picture by Mr Burne-Jones. Guilty Love, captured and tortured by the famous women whom he has betrayed, is crucified to a tree in a dark grove of myrtles, and tormented there by the wrathful ladies, until Venus his mother pushes her way through the throng, and more enraged than they, lashes her son's pale limbs with wreaths of thorny roses, till they are stained with purple. The opening lines seem to me so delicate and felicitous, so suggestive of the road which English poetry might have taken, that I venture to quote them, the more as the volume in which they were printed is almost inaccessible :—

"In the aery fields by Maro's muse display'd,
Where myrtle groves the frantic lovers shade,
The heroines their orgies celebrate,
And past occasions of their deaths relate;
As in a spreading wood scarce pierc'd by day,
They 'mongst thin reeds and drooping poppy stray,
By stainless lakes, and rivers without noise
Upon whose banks sad flowers, by names of boys
And kings once known, i' the cloudy twilight wither,
Self-lov'd Narcissus, Hyacinth, together
With Crocus golden-haired, Adonis drest
In purple, Ajax with a sigh impressed."

He is not less softly musical, not less enthralled by the spirit of his model, when he comes to translate the *Vigil of Venus*, with its delicious recurrent refrain—

"Cras amet qui nunquam amavit, quique amavit cras amet"—

perhaps the most modern, the most unclassical touch that antique literature has bequeathed to us[1].

It is characteristic of a too obstinate pleasure in literature of this sort, that it deprives its votaries

---

[1] I cannot resist the temptation to refer to the charming fancies which Mr Pater has woven around this poem in his new romance, *Marius the Epicurean*. I hope it is not frivolous to wish that our learned and exquisite Stanley could have enjoyed these ingenious volumes.

of the power to rise to graver and more manly studies. Stanley cannot be stigmatized with this fault as a scholar, for he rose to a great attainment in his once celebrated *History of Greek Philosophy;* but as a poet he showed something of this weakness. The translations appeared in 1649; in 1651 he published his original poems, and they were disappointing. We see in them the intellectual faults which led him to exaggerate the value of writers like Ausonius. If Waller met with them at Paris, he would be sagacious enough to lay them down with the remark that their author was no serious opponent of his system in poetry. They belong to a class which was already out of fashion when Stanley was a child. They are lyrics of the elaborate kind, mostly in extremely artificial metres, which were in vogue among the cavalier poets of the Court of Whitehall. They are of the kindred of Carew and Lovelace, of Habington and Suckling, but they possess a sort of cold refinement which those brocaded lyrists would have disdained. I have remarked elsewhere that in no poet of the century is the negative quality of shrinking from ugliness and coarseness so defined as in Stanley, the world in which his fancy loved to wander being one of refined Arcadian beauty, rather chilly and autumnal, but inhabited by groups of nymphs and shepherds, who hung garlands of flowers on votive urns, or took hands in stately, pensive dances[1].

As the century declined, the efforts at a poetical reaction became rapidly fewer, less sincere, and less apparent[2]. We need not stop to examine the work of Vaughan, the Silurist, the last survivor of the sacred school of Cambridge poets of whom Herbert is the best known. It was an accident that Vaughan lived on until the last decade of the century. His lovely occasional pieces, "Happy those early days when I" and "They are all gone into the world of light," are contained in most collections. Vaughan belongs to the survival, not to the reaction. John Norris of Bemerton, on the other hand, a direct

---

[1] The same year which saw the publication of Stanley's *Poems* witnessed that of the one volume which he can be said to have inspired, the *Salmacis, Lyrian and Sylvia, Forsaken Lydia and the Rape of Helen*, of Edward Sherburne. From Sherburne, who dedicates his volume to Stanley, we learn that the latter was equally fluent in Greek, Latin, Italian, French and Spanish.

[2] To enter into any discussion here of the vexed question of the authorship of *Thealma and Clearchus*, 1683, would lead me too far afield. I have myself no doubt whatever that Izaak Walton was the author of this poem, and "John Chalkhill" a half-myth, that is to say a real person dead and forgotten so long before as not to endanger Walton's harmless mystification. At the same time, it was certainly not in May 1678, but probably thirty or thirty-five years earlier that, as Walton would have us believe, "the Author died, and I hope the Reader will be sorry." Flatman's poem has, I think, been overlooked as a contemporary testimony to Walton's authorship.

G.   14

imitator of the Marinists, designed nothing less than a revolution when, so late as 1678, he brought out his *Miscellanies*. He says in the preface to the reader: "The design of the present undertaking is to restore the declining genius of poetry to its primitive and genuine greatness, to wind up the strings of the Muses' lyre, and to show that sense and gracefulness are as consistent in these as in any other compositions. I design here all the masculine sense and argument of a dissertation, with the advantage of poetic fineness, beauty, and spirit." Norris, however, was read for his piety, not for his poetry, and his own remark about most religious verse, that it is "stiff, flat, and insipid," is not belied by any flexibility or elevation in his own odes and canticles.

The very last effort made to restore romantic poetry to its old place in English literature, however, was made in 1687, the year that Waller died, by a certain Philip Ayres, who published a volume of *Lyric Poems,* mostly from the Italian and Spanish, in the preface to which he spoke respectfully of the prestige of "Mr Waller, Mr Cowley, and Mr Dryden," but hoped that he would not be thought presumptuous if, in spite of their great example, he himself recurred to the manner of writing indulged in by "the famous Mr Spenser,

Sir Philip Sidney, and Mr Milton." Ayres is remarkable as almost the only English sonneteer between Milton and Gray, but his sonnets, though sometimes singularly learned and precise in form, are seldom otherwise interesting. His book enjoyed no success, and we know nothing of his career, except that he was a personal friend of Dryden, and an excellent scholar.

I have, however, still to present the greatest and the most interesting of the poets who wrote during the Commonwealth in opposition to Waller and his followers. The name of Andrew Marvell is illustrious wherever political purity is valued, wherever intellectual liberty is defended. To dwell upon the qualities of a character so candid, and upon the virtues of so single-minded a patriot, may seem out of place in a disquisition on the rise of classical poetry in England, but this patriot, this exquisite citizen, was a poet also, and a poet worthy of his civic reputation. Nor was there anything inconsistent in the fact that a man whose hands were pure in an age of universal corruption, and who put the interests of the people first when public virtue had scarcely been discovered, should be a romantic idealist when he came to put his innermost thoughts down in metre. Marvell is nothing if not consistent, and we find the same brain and heart engaged with rustic visions at Nunappleton and with the anger of statecraft at Westminster.

Dr Grosart discovered that Andrew Marvell was born at Winestead in Yorkshire on the 31st of March, 1621. His father, a Puritan divine, was translated to the wider field of a parish in Hull when his son was four years old, and eventually to the Mastership of the grammar-school there. The future poet lived at Hull under the paternal roof until he was fifteen. Whether he was very severely kept in check all that time may be doubted; his antagonist, Bishop Parker, in future years, accused him of having consorted with "boatswains and cabin-boys" along the tarry quays of Hull, and he may have thus early acquired that remarkable flow of bad language which makes his satires somewhat distressingly remarkable.

Like almost all the poets of the age, Marvell received his education at Cambridge. His father had belonged to the puritan college of Emmanuel, but the poet came to Trinity, whither he entered, just too late to be at the University with Milton, Cowley, or Waller, in 1633. While he was at Trinity, some men at Peterhouse, who were tools of the Jesuits, inveigled him over to Rome, and actually, it would appear, smuggled the boy up to one of their secret seminaries in London. The story is, that his father had scent of this, and following his son up to town, found him in a bookseller's shop, captured him, and brought him, restored to the Church of England, safely back to Trinity. The case was by no means a solitary one at Cambridge, and the practice of the Jesuits was so alarming to parents, as indeed it well might be, that there was talk of passing a bill through Star Chamber to deal with it.

Andrew Marvell lost his admirable father in 1640, just before he himself left college. The circumstances of the death were romantic and have often been repeated. The worthy puritan set sail to cross the Humber in company with a lady, and with "a young beautiful couple who were going to be wedded." The day was calm and fair, but Mr Marvell had so strong a presentiment of death that he spoke of it cheerfully to those whom he left, and even threw his staff ashore, exclaiming, "Ho! for heaven!" The friends were only half way across the estuary, when a sudden storm arose, upset the boat, and utterly destroyed the whole party, no remains either of the vessel or of the passengers being ever recovered. It is said that the mother of the young lady who was thus untimely drowned consoled herself by a whimsical act of generosity, and that Marvell being left an orphan through the accident, she sent for him from college, and adopted him as her son. It is probable that the munificence of this lady, who was a near relative of Milton's friend Cyriack Skinner, supplied the young man with the funds needful to support him in France, Holland, Spain, and Italy for the next six years.

It may well be that Mrs Skinner, although she was able to support him during her lifetime, was unable to provide for her protégé after her death. At all events we find him in 1650 earning his livelihood as the tutor of Mary Fairfax, afterwards Duchess of Buckingham. This little maid, daughter of the great Lord Fairfax, was in her twelfth year at the time, and it appears that Marvell lived as her teacher in the house at Nunappleton for two years. This home of the Fairfaxes was a mansion romantically situated at the junction of the Ouse and the Wharfe, in the lowlands of Yorkshire, and on the very site of an ancient Cistercian nunnery. There can be very little doubt that the greater part of Marvell's lyrical poems were written at this house, from his twenty-ninth to his thirty-first year, in the beautiful seclusion from which Milton's famous letter called him, as by the blast of a trumpet. The neighbourhood of Nunappleton was all given up to

"fragrant gardens, shady woods,
Deep meadows and transparent floods,"
and its flowery wildernesses and rich grassy fields inspired the remarkable series of lyrics to which we must now give our attention.

The world is seldom told at what stray and occasional moments, how hurriedly, and again how seldom, a poet's inspiration flows. It may well be that the music lies frozen at a young man's heart until some peculiar condition in his circumstances, a chain of emotions called forth by some peaceful and novel situation, melts it into sudden poetry. In a few months, perhaps, the conditions change, the mind is released from its tension, and he has written in that short time most of what is to introduce him to posterity as a poet. In ages of general political disorder, and of civic and personal insecurity, this must particularly be the case. We know for how long a time the muse of Milton was silenced by public and private anxieties, and we should be ignorant of one great section of his genius, of his romantic and melodious power in lyrical writing, if it had not been for his retirement at Horton. What Horton was to Milton, Nunappleton was to Marvell, it made a lyrical poet of him.

This series of verses was carefully preserved by

his widow, and given to the world, with other of his pieces, in a small folio, in 1681. A fine copy of this rare book is one of the most dainty and desirable of all English publications from the Restoration to the end of the century. It is not quite complete, and notably the celebrated Horatian Ode on Oliver Cromwell is not included in it,— Mrs Marvell did not trouble herself with any poems but those which she possessed in her husband's handwriting,—but it is still the most luxurious shape in which Marvell's poems can be read. The Nunappleton pieces are strewed over it without any attempt at arrangement, and the one which holds the key to the rest is printed last. This is a long poem in praise of the house, written in eight-line stanzas of octo-syllabic verse, and extending to nearly eight hundred lines. Any student who wishes to understand Marvell must read this long and difficult piece with care. He will soon see that he has to deal with what Dr. Johnson called a "metaphysical," and what I have ventured to call a "Marinist" poet of the most extreme order.

Marvell is the last of the school of Donne, and in several respects he comes nearer to the master than any of his precursors. Certain conceits of Donne's, for instance that one about the lover and the pair of compasses[1], are often quoted as examples of a monstrous class. We get to think of Donne as exclusively the forger of tawdry false jewellery such as this, "rime's sturdy cripple," as Coleridge ingeniously calls him. But Donne was also the writer of lines and passages that speak so directly to the heart and to the senses that those who have come under 'their spell feel a sort of shyness in quoting them; they are so personal that to discuss them seems an indiscretion. Something of the same odd reserve seems due in the reader of some of Shakespeare's *Sonnets*, of some of Coleridge's shorter poems. I cannot, myself, bear to hear poetry of this intimate kind analyzed or even touched by unsympathetic people. This is a feeling which may not be praiseworthy in the

---

[1]   "If they be two, they are two so
        As stiff twin compasses are two,
   Thy soul, the fix'd foot, makes no show
      To move, but doth, if th' other do.

   And though it in the centre sit,
      Yet when the other far doth roam,
   It leans and hearkens after it,
      And grows erect as that comes home.

   Such wilt thou be to me, who must
      Like th' other foot, obliquely run,
   Thy firmness makes my circle just,
      And makes me end where I begun."
           A Valediction forbidding Mourning.

student, but it is a proof of extraordinary felicity, mingled with sincerity, in the style of the writer so discussed or touched. There can be no doubt that Donne possesses this quality, denied perhaps to all his scholars, until revealed again, in a certain measure, in Marvell. The note, however, is not so sharply struck in him as in Donne; there is more suavity and grace. The conceits are perhaps as wild. Here is one :—

> "Love wisely had of long foreseen
>   That he must once grow old,
> And therefore stored a magazine,
>   To save him from the cold.
> He kept the several cells replete
>   With nitre thrice refined,
> The naphtha's and the sulphur's heat,
>   And all that burns the mind."

This terrible magazine, which is fortified by a double gate, and which would have enflamed the whole of nature if one spark had fallen into it, turns out to be—the heart of Celia. Again, whole stanzas in the Nunappleton poem are taken up with a description of the garden as a military camp, through which the bee beats his drum, while the flowers are soldiers, who fire off volleys of perfume, and stand at parade, under their various colours, in stately regiments all day long :—

> "But when the vigilant patrol
> Of stars walks round about the pole,
> Their leaves that to their stalks are curled,
> Seem to their staves the ensigns furled.
> Then in some flower's belovèd hut
> Each bee as sentinel is shut,
> And sleeps so too, but if once stirr'd
> She runs you thro' or asks the word."

This is pretty and harmless, but perhaps just because it errs so gently against the canons of style, we ask ourselves how so seriously-minded a man as Marvell could run on in such a childish way. There is a good deal in Marvell that is of this species of wit, graceful and coloured, but almost infantile. Waller and Denham had taught English people to outgrow these childish toys of fancy, and if there had been nothing more than this in Marvell, we should not be regarding him as a serious element in the reaction. But there is a great deal more, and allowing the conceits to be taken for granted, we may inquire into the character of what is best in his lyrics.

In the long Nunappleton poem, then, and in that celebrated piece which is printed now in most collections of English poetry, *The Garden*, we find a personal sympathy with nature, and particularly with vegetation, which was quite a novel thing, and which found no second exponent until Wordsworth came forward with his still wider and more philosophical commerce with the inanimate world. For flowers, trees, and grasses, Marvell expresses a sort of personal passion. They stand between him and humanity, they are to him "forms more real than living man." He calls upon the woodlands of Nunappleton to save him from the noisy world:—

> "Bind me, ye woodbines, in your twines,
> Curl me about, ye gadding vines,
> And oh! so close your circles lace
> That I may never leave this place."

Again he says:—

> "How safe, methinks, and strong, behind
> These trees have I encamped my mind,"

and he repeats this sentiment of the security of natural solitude again and again. His style, when he can put his conceits behind him, is extremely sharp and delicate, with a distinction of phrase that is quite unknown to most of his contemporaries. To praise "The Garden" or "Bermudas" would be an impertinence; but I think few readers know what charming and unique poetry lies hid in the series of poems in which Marvell writes as a

Mower, with a fantastical regret for the flowers and grasses that he cuts down. He says:—

> "I am the mower Damon, known
> Through all the meadows I have mown,
> On me the morn her dew distils
> Before her darling daffodils."

He declares a profound passion for a possible Juliana, but it is really the wood-moths gleaming on the bark, the vigilant heron in its nest at the top of the ash-tree, the garish eye of the new-hatched throstle staring through the hazels, that hold his poetical affections. He is the last of the English romantic poets for several generations, and no one of them all, early or late, has regarded nature with a quicker or more loving attention than he. He is an alien indeed among the men of periwigs and ruffles.

THE RESTORATION.

THE RESTORATION.

WE have now reached the year of that event which occupied so many lyres and awakened so many darts and flames in poetic bosoms, namely, the restitution of the monarchy, the return of the exiled Stuart as King Charles the Second. This date, 1660, is usually given in text-books of literature as marking the commencement of the change to the classical style. As well might we call the platform of the railway-station at St Lazare the point of division between England and France. In 1660 the journey was complete, the change was made. Not one of the odes and pæans which welcomed the Stuarts back, but proved, by the internal evidence of each of its lines, that the old order of poetry had given way to the new. Perhaps not in all cases was the panegyrist conscious of his voice; sometimes he may even have supposed himself to greet Charles II. in the accents dear to the court of Charles I. In vain; the new form compelled him, the new order of ideas inspired him. That worthy Conservative woman, the

Matchless Orinda, with every desire to be writing in the good old Royalist way as Donne and Herrick wrote, snatches her lyre and strikes the rebellious strings. This is the sort of music which they utter:—

> "You justly may forsake a land which you
> Have found so guilty and so fatal too;
> Fortune injurious to your innocence
> Shot all her poison'd arrows here, or hence[1]."

We need no more; we see that Waller has bewitched her, that she is totally ensnared.

It may be that my readers have been awaiting the introduction of a great name into this discourse, which hitherto has scarcely been mentioned. I may be asked, where is Dryden, the accredited source and leader of the classical movement? My answer is, that in tracing the rise of that movement, and in examining its early development, I do not discover the influence of Dryden. In guiding the movement when it was once organized, in lending to it the force and prestige of his commanding genius, in forging the distich anew and in directing it as a missile is directed by a powerful machine, in all this Dryden took a foremost part, but he was not an inventor or a primal force in the new

[1] *To the Queen Mother's Majesty*, ll 1—4. Jan. 1, 1661.

scheme. When in the course of events he began to follow it, he was long attracted to the most volatile part of it, the heresy of Cowley. A glance at dates is here most valuable. Dryden was born in 1631, more than a quarter of a century later than Waller; he was but a child when the epoch-making volumes of the school were published, and when at last he began himself to be a poet,—for he was slow and laborious in development,—he came forward as the most absurd of Marinists. His lines on the death of Lord Hastings have supplied matter for mirth to critic after critic; the terrible series of similes by which the symptoms of the smallpox are described, are well known, and offensive beyond measure. Here is a less hackneyed fragment, in which Dryden plays with the notion that Lord Hastings' death was premature:—

> "Thus fades the oak in the spring, in the blade the corn,
> Thus, without young, this phœnix dies, new born!
> Must then old three-legged grey-beards, with their gout,
> Catarrhs, rheums, achës, live three ages out?
> Time's offals, only fit for the hospital,
> Or to hang an antiquary's rooms withal."

In taste, in language, above all in versification, this belongs to the first decades of the century; it is almost Elizabethan. Dryden's next departure was in the direction of Davenant, whose *Gondibert* affected him to the exclusion of almost every other influence in the *Heroic Stanzas* of 1659[1], and in the *Annus Mirabilis* of 1666. In his *Astræa Redux* he is feeling after the new prosody, with only doubtful success, and his verse is first worthy to be named with that of Waller and Denham in the *Coronation Panegyric*. But by this time the Restoration was already a part of history, and we feel that Dryden, as Eusden said,

"Faintly distinguished in his thirtieth year,"

is by no means to be counted among those who led the van of classicism. Of course a man so intelligent and so worldly as he would not long resist the dominant stream of his generation. Milton, awakening from his long indifference to verse, might disdain to observe the change in taste which had taken place; but Dryden was of a temperament less sublime and less austere, and his finger was ever upon the pulse of public feeling, guiding it, indeed, in one sense, but none the less directed by it in another.

It is time, however, if Dryden is excluded from our attention in this place, for us to turn to those

---

[1] It is noticeable that in this, his earliest publication, Dryden was associated with Sprat and with the veteran Waller.

writers of far less genius than he who preceded him and made a road for him. And chiefly Waller, whose name has been so frequently repeated by us; and who has now for a long time been left in the background. We saw that his mother, the clever woman at Beaconsfield, had carried those amiable pleasantries of hers with her awful cousin, the Protector, to a point where the throwing of a napkin over her head at the dinner-table seemed scarcely chastisement enough. Oliver Cromwell lost his temper with her at last; Mrs Waller was requested to pay her daughter, Mrs Scroope, a visit, and to let it be a permanent one. The poet's mother, in fact, became a prisoner in her son-in-law's house, and though gifted with no small share of her son's brazen and irrepressible assurance, she seems to have felt that it was time for a change of tactics. We do not know the terms upon which she, and presently Edmund Waller, also, made peace with the Commonwealth, nor how the poet contrived to temper this second act of apparent treachery to his Queen and their common friends.

In spite of our romantic confidence in the chivalry of our ancestors, it is certain that personal honour was not regarded as we regard it now. Waller had lost no caste with his own party by his pusillanimous confessions in 1643; he found no want of warmth among the Roundheads when he ratted to them in 1654. Among the pencil memoranda taken in the House of Commons during the Long Parliament, by Sir Ralph Verney, there is this astounding entry, namely, that Waller, from his place in the House, remarked on Tuesday, the 23rd of June, 1642, "Let us look first to our safety, and then to our honour." Nobody seems to have been shocked, although subsequent speakers expressed a different view regarding the duty of parliament. We may gauge the difference between now and then, and in so doing excuse a little the apparent worthlessness of Waller's morality, by imagining the uproar which such a sentiment would nowadays create in any representative body of legislators in the world.

Another phrase of Waller's, casually noted down by Sir Ralph Verney, is also perhaps worthy of citation as throwing light upon the poet's character and position. When the ire of the Long Parliament was roused by Palmer's protestation, Waller rose and said, "Let no man be punished for temperance, lest we seem to punish virtue." This was the voice of the neutral, of the scholarly man who saw right on both sides, and who would fain be friends with both. No one could be further removed from such treasonable fickleness as history attributes to Waller than the late Dean Stanley. Yet his known character may help us to realize a character like Waller's. Very intelligent and pacific, at heart a little sceptical about the merits of tweedledum and tweedledee, it is difficult for this class of man to take a firm position between two virulent and hostile camps. He loves the individuals in both, he sees much to hallow a sacrifice of prejudice on the one hand and on the other. Waller, at all events, could move from the friendship of Henrietta Maria to the friendship of Oliver Cromwell without a twinge of conscience.

It must be admitted that Waller carries that breadth of view, that power of seeing both sides of a question, which Sir Arthur Helps so ingeniously defended, to a bold extreme. His boldness, indeed, is his best excuse. During the Civil War, he had extolled Charles I. as "a mixture of divinity and love," and a chain "on which the fabric of our world depends." Oliver Cromwell found it expedient to cut off the head of this paragon, and rule England in his place. Waller obtains pardon, and returns home with a panegyric to the Protector, in which he remarks that

"With such a chief the meanest nation blest
 Might hope to lift her head above the rest."

Cromwell dies, and Waller immediately indites a third poem, to his son Richard, the new Protector, in which he says:—

> "Ungrateful we, if we no tears allow
> To him that gave us peace and empire too."

A few months later the Stuarts are reinstated, and Waller's Muse this fourth time sings out in equally clear and unmistakable notes of welcome to Charles II.:—

> "Faith, Law and Piety, that banished train,
> Justice and Truth, with you return again."

This seems, perhaps, mere cowardly shiftiness, like that of

> "A peach that's got the yallers
> With the meanness busting out,"

as Mr Lowell would say; but our scorn turns into astonishment when we find the unabashed poet publishing the four successive poems in the same volume of his acknowledged verse. Even in those days, so broad a sympathy could not escape without comment, and when Waller presented the fourth of these panegyrics to Charles II. the King made the awkward remark that he thought it much inferior to his panegyric on Cromwell. This double thrust, attacking his loyalty and his poetry at once, would have silenced most men, but Waller extricated himself from the trying position with his habitual coolness. "Sir!" he replied, "we poets never succeed so well in writing truth as fiction." The retort is one of the most nimble in all the history of wit, if we remember the terrible occasion upon which it was made, and the still-existing doubt as to whose head should and whose head should not remain upon rebellious but repentant shoulders.

The King was perfectly right. The poem on Cromwell is far superior to that on Charles II., although it bears all the signs of a superior sincerity. It contains some beautiful passages, as eloquent as any which Dryden was able to compose twenty years later, smooth sometimes with the suavity of Pope himself. Let us remember that these graceful couplets were composed as early as 1654:—

> "Your drooping country, torn with civil hate,
> Restored by you, is made a glorious state,
> The seat of empire, where the Irish come,
> And the unwilling Scot, to fetch their doom;
> The sea's our own, and now all nations greet
> With bending sails each vessel of our fleet;
> Our power extends as far as winds can blow,
> Or swelling sails around the globe may go;

·Heaven, that has placed this island to give law,
To balance Europe, and her states to awe,
In this conjunction does on Britain smile,
The greatest leader, and the greatest isle.
Whether this portion of the world were rent
By the rude ocean from the continent,
Or, thus created,—sure it was designed.
To be the second refuge of mankind."

The execution of these verses is nearly perfect; the only point at which criticism can detect their immaturity being the tendency which they have to form themselves into groups of four lines. This is the haunting echo of the old stanzaic form, which Dryden himself was very slow to lose. The secret, as it appears to me, of that apparently extravagant eulogy which Dryden paid to Oldham at his early death, in 1684, greeting him as "the Marcellus of our tongue," a tribute which has been a stumbling-block to many readers of Oldham's particularly uninspired verses, rests in this, that Oldham was the first to liberate himself, in the use of the distich, from this under-current of a stanza, and to write heroic verse straight on, couplet by couplet, ascending by steady strides and not by irregular leaps[1]. In Pope's best satires we see this art carried

[1] Any one who will venture to read Oldham's disagreeable *Satire upon the Jesuits*, written in 1679, will see the truth of this

to its final perfection; after his time the connecting link between couplet and couplet became lost, and at last in the decline poems became, as someone has said, mere cases of lancets lying side by side. But in Dryden's day the connection was still only too obvious, and it strikes me that it may have been from a consciousness of this defect, that Dryden adopted that triplet, with a final alexandrine, which he is so fond of introducing. If so, he attempted to cure a small error by committing a greater one.

The life of Waller has not been attempted since the art of biography has been understood in its modern sense. It would not be impossible to write it, for a great number of allusions to him, anecdotes and ana illustrating his position, exist in various memoirs of the times. He was popular at court during the reign of Charles II., petted by the King and by the great ladies, and as he slowly grew an old man in that atmosphere of polite diversion, his position increased in dignity. He was, without a peer, the reigning wit at Charles's court, and various stories are told in illustration of his vivacity.

It was noted as a thing almost unique in those

remark, and note the effect that its versification had upon that series of Dryden's satires which immediately followed it.

days, that Mr Waller was a water-drinker. We cannot easily realize how perilous was the position of a man who refused to drink with his friends in the seventeenth century. He was liable to insult, and even to personal attack, for to refuse to share a bottle of wine was to inflict a wound upon the honour of the man who offered it. Waller had the courage to stick to water, merely, I imagine, because he had observed that wine disagreed with him[1]. It is recorded that the King did not on this account exclude him from his company, since Waller "had the dexterity to accommodate his discourse to the pitch of the others' as it sunk." George Savile, Lord Halifax, the famous *viveur*, and a pupil of Waller's in verse, said that there was only one man in England he would allow to stay in the same room with him unless he drank, and that was Ned Waller.

The poet's universal popularity led him to imagine that there was nothing which he could not get for the asking, and so when the Provostship of Eton fell vacant in 1665 he begged for that, with some effrontery. The easy monarch had no objection, and gave him the grant, but the Earl of

---

[1] "Waller had but a tender, weak body, but was always very temperate. Made him damnable drunk at Somerset House, when at the water stairs he fell down and had a cruel fall. 'Twas a pity to use such a sweet swan so inhumanly." *Aubrey.*

Clarendon, as Lord Chancellor, refused to seal it, the statutes of the college then absolutely excluding laymen from the office of provost. Waller considered that his old friend should have waived this difficulty, and he had the meanness to lie in wait for an opportunity for revenge. In the course of two years it came. Waller sat in Parliament, as member for Hastings, from 1661 to 1678, and when, in 1667, the Duke of Buckingham brought forward the prosecution of the Earl of Clarendon, Waller supported his motion in the House of Commons, and both voted and spoke for the impeachment of the great historian. It is not to be wondered at that the portrait Clarendon gives of Waller,—and this portrait is that by which posterity knows him best,—should be painted in none of the brightest colours.

It appears that as Waller grew older all the pleasure which he might reasonably have extracted from his wealth, honours, and influence was soured and spoiled for him by this craving desire to be made Provost of Eton. Having removed Lord Clarendon out of the way, he thought that he might be more successful in grasping the prize when Dr Allestre died in 1668. Accordingly he moved heaven and earth to be elected, but again without effect, for the fellows unanimously gave their votes for Dr Zachary Cradock. Waller would not sit down under his defeat. He wearied the King with his complaints, till Charles II. consented to bring the matter before Privy Council. For three days the most noted lawyers of the age argued in Star Chamber on the point whether the King had the power to alter the statutes of Eton College in such a way as to indulge Mr Waller's whim. The Bishop of Lincoln had to be called in to negative the poet's pretensions, and at last it was decided that it was impossible to allow the King to stultify his own laws.

Waller sulked a little, but finally determined not to retire into country life. For more than a quarter of a century he was one of the fashionable figures of London, inhabiting a fine town-house on the west side of St James's Street, where he entertained a good deal, and received the homage of men of letters. In 1671 he was nominated one of the original lords commissioners of plantations, thus leading off the long list of men of letters who have been officially connected with the Board of Trade. His parliamentary career was broken only by his death, for when the House was dissolved in 1678, he was immediately returned for Chipping Wycombe, which he represented until, in 1685, he was returned for Saltash in Cornwall in James II.'s only parliament. Altogether, he sat in the House of Commons for five-and-forty years; I suppose that there is no other prominent English writer, except Mr Gladstone, of whom the same can be said. Waller's views of his duties as a representative, however, were by no means those of to-day; he spoke frequently, and on a wide range of subjects, but although his delivery was singularly good, and his speeches eloquent, it was remarked that he delighted the House more by the grace of his discourse than by the weight of his argument[1].

Whether we must attribute it to the water-drinking or no is not for me to decide, but it is certain that Waller showed a rare elasticity of body and mind to a great old age. As a politician it is claimed that he was privy to the intrigues of the Revolution, and that he sent his son as an envoy with valuable help to the Prince of Orange. James II.'s policy disgusted him, and he urged those about him not to prop up the Stuarts, but let the King "be left high and dry like a stranded whale."

[1] Thomas Rymer says of him, in his *Elegy*:—

"From James to James they count him o'er and o'er
In four successive reigns a senator;
On him, amidst the legislative throng,
Their eyes and ears and every heart they hung;
Within those walls if we Apollo knew,
Less could he warm, nor throw a shaft so true;
What life, what lightning, blanched around the Chair!
It was no House, if Waller was not there."

This must have been in the very last months of his life, and he did not live to see his prediction verified. In 1686, however, when he was eighty-one, he showed an intellectual vitality[1], or rejuvenescence, which, in its kind, is almost unparalleled. He sat down to write a long poem, in the couplet he had invented, on the subject of *Divine Love*. This work yields to none of his younger productions in grace, thoughtfulness, or melody, though perhaps it has a touch of the languor of age. Marvellous to record, he completed the poem, and when he could write no more, dictated, just before he died, these beautiful lines as an appendix to his aged labours:—

> "When I for age could neither read nor write,
> The subject made me able to indite;
> The soul, with nobler resolutions decked,
> The body stooping, does herself erect:
> No mortal parts are requisite to raise
> Her, that unbodied can her Maker praise.

[1] I do not know whether Saint-Evremond's epigram on Waller's old age has ever been reprinted. It was written in 1684, and appeared in 1688 in *Poems to the Memory of that Incomparable Poet Edmund Waller*.
> "Waller, qui ne sait rien des maux de la vieillesse,
> Dont la vivacité fait honte aux jeunes gens,
> S'attache à la beauté pour vivre plus long temps,
> Et ce qu'on nommerait dans un autre faiblesse,
> Est en ce rare esprit une sage tendresse,
> Qui le fait résister à l'injure des ans."

The seas are quiet, when the winds give o'er!
So calm are we, when passions are no more!
For then we know how vain it was to boast
Of fleeting things, so certain to be lost.
Clouds of affection[1] from our younger eyes
Conceal that emptiness which age descries;
The soul's dark cottage, batter'd and decay'd,
Lets in new light, thro' chinks that time has made;
Stronger by weakness, wiser, men become,
As they draw near to their eternal home;
Leaving the old, both worlds at once they view,
That stand upon the threshold of the new."

These were his last lines, composed, tradition declares, when he was already on his death-bed; and all that cynicism itself can object against them is, that the aged courtier, who had never failed in tact, approaches the confines of eternity with all the solemnity and decorum that such a step demanded. A little while before this event, he had the whim to buy a small estate at Coleshill, where he was born; he liked to go over there to dine, and once being carried to it, he said he should be glad to die there, like the stag, when he was roused. But his fatal dropsy happened to seize him at one of his other mansions, that at Beaconsfield. The King's surgeon was called in, and told him that he must die, whereupon, as it is said, the old man

---

[1] That is to say, of *prejudice*.

composed those verses of adieu to life which I have just quoted. He was spared a long illness, and died very composedly, with all his children and his retainers around him, on the 21st of October, 1687, being half-way across his eighty-third year.

The serenity of the close of Waller's life contrasts in a singular degree with the pain and agitation which marked the last years of his first pupil and fellow-labourer, Sir John Denham. The poet of *Cooper's Hill* was among those who crept back to England unobserved during Cromwell's protectorate. As early as 1652 he returned, and having lost all his fortune by gaming and the wars, he was entertained as a guest at Wilton House, by the Earl of Pembroke, for a year. He lived, very modestly, by the practice of architecture, until the Restoration, keeping his eye upon the office of Surveyor-General of His Majesty's Buildings, which Charles I. had promised him in succession to Inigo Jones. When that famous architect died, in 1652, Denham was with Charles II. at St Germains, and he received a nominal appointment to the post. What claims he had as an artist I have been unable to discover[1];

[1] Evelyn disagreed with him about the site for Greenwich Palace, and after an interview on the 19th of October 1661 came away, "knowing Sir John to be a better poet than architect, though he had Mr Webb (Inigo Jones's man) to assist him." This was John Webb (1611—1672), who designed the scenery for the *Siege of Rhodes*, and built a good many of the buildings often carelessly attributed to Inigo Jones.

he is said to have designed part of Burlington House, but in association with Sir Christopher Wren, and the front of Greenwich Hospital, but from the designs of Inigo Jones.

All this, however, came to pass at the Restoration, when after a long period of poverty, Denham felt the warmth of prosperity again. At the coronation of Charles II. he was knighted. The last twenty years of his life, as far as we can perceive, were darkened by domestic suffering. He had married a young and pretty wife, who had the misfortune to attract the Duke of York's admiration, and not virtue enough to resist it[1]. This preyed so much upon the poet's senses, that he became insane, and continued in this condition till near the end of his life. He recovered, however, and continued to be the King's Surveyor till his death on March 19, 1668[2]. Denham was a most unpopular man.

[1] Lady Denham died suddenly on the 6th of January, 1667, while under the protection of the Duke of York. It was supposed that she was poisoned, and Marvell says, in *The Last Instructions to a Painter*:—

"What frosts to fruits, what arsenic to a rat,
 Was to fair Denham mortal chocolate."

[2] In many text-books the date of Denham's death is given as 1688. But for reasons given below this seems highly improbable, although by far the most accurate account of him, that in the *Biographia Britannica*, gives the latter year. From contemporary records I have collected a few dates which help us to follow the course of Denham's life. Wren was made his associate in 1662.

Many of his contemporaries speak of him personally with contempt or aversion. He was accused of violence and discourtesy in his manner to ladies; of stinginess and trickery in business; of robbing the King in the practice of his profession, and even of stealing or buying from others the poems to which he owed his fame. The last accusation we may lightly dismiss; the others, it is to be hoped, are no better founded; but Denham leaves upon us the impression of an unamiable man. He died worth £7,000, and this in spite of the interval of his insanity.

Denham's last verses were pronounced at Poets' Corner, when Cowley was buried in Westminster Abbey in August 1667, so that, if he died early in

From 1664 Denham and Wren were entrusted with the repairing of St Paul's. On the 21st February 1665 Pepys dined with Denham, who was evidently perfectly well, at the Lord Chancellor's new house. The poet-architect's house was in Scotland Yard, whither he took his bride, Margaret Brook, when he married her on the 25th of May 1665. In the early part of 1666 the Duke of York's attentions to Lady Denham became marked; in the summer she yields to them, and Denham becomes mad. In 1668 Pepys hears a rumour of his death, which rumour may or may not be true, but has no doubt introduced that date into the text-books. On the other hand, the well-informed writer in the *Biographia Britannica*, after speaking of Denham's madness, goes on to say that "recovering from that disorder, he continued in great esteem at court, and with all persons of taste, until he died at his office near Whitehall, in March 1688." His long-continued madness might account for the absence of his name after 1667 from memoirs of the Times, but Wren seems to have stepped into Denham's office in 1668.

the next year, his madness must have lasted a very little while. Waller survived him nearly twenty years, and it is curious that if he had but lived a month or two longer he might have been alive with Pope, and have linked his generation with the generation of Shakespeare, into which Waller was born. This extraordinary extension of Waller's life had another consequence, namely, that he survived a number of poets much younger than himself, who had grown up, as it were, at his feet, and who cannot be thought of except as supporters of his poetical system. Among these the most celebrated names are those of Oldham, Roscommon, Otway, Rochester, and Buckingham.

Having thus wound up the threads of the purely historical part of our inquiry, let us turn to the critical part. What was the new gift in poetry, what was its force, and what its attraction? This dry and urban manner of writing, so precise, colourless, and impersonal, what was the secret of its fascination? To us, as a poetical form, it is apt to seem as insipid as a letter written by a child whose nursery-governess has directed the pen and suggested the expressions. In the earlier of these chapters I have partly answered these questions. The fascination lay to a great degree in contrast. The child had so long run wild in garden and orchard that to be brushed and cleaned, and to sit up to table at its lessons, had all the attraction of a new kind of play. When a mortal, now and then in the course of the centuries, lights upon a new form of writing, the charm of it is irresistible. The trouble is but to be inspired with something truly original, and then all the world troops to it like a flight of moths.

Some curious facts may be observed to show how difficult it was to resist the new distich, and how right and proper it seemed that it should be adopted. Herrick, the most romantic of poets, with a throat like a mocking-bird's, capable of all the ingenuities of metre and measure, writes a few lines of personal compliment[1] to a leader in the opposite camp, to Denham; and for once in his life, merely because he has been reading *Cooper's Hill*, and the invisible bird-lime has caught him, he writes those lines in excellent distich. Instances of the fact that people began, soon after the introduction of the new form, to be unable to endure the old prosody,

---

[1] "Or looked I back unto the times hence flown
To praise those muses, and dislike our own?
Or did I walk those pæan gardens through,
To kick the flowers, or scorn their odours too?
I might, and justly, be reputed here,
One nicely mad or peevishly sincere."

No one would suspect that these lines were written by the songbird of the *Hesperides*.

even in works where they were accustomed to it, are numerous. There were complaints of the unreadableness of *The Faery Queen*, and an anonymous hand re-wrote it in 1687, "with the obsolete language, and manner of verse completely laid aside, and delivered in heroick numbers" for polite readers. But perhaps even more odd than this is a feat which Waller himself performed, the alteration of the close of Beaumont and Fletcher's *Maid's Tragedy*, which all the world knew in blank verse, into distich. It was no longer tolerable to indite such a vulgar thing as blank verse, and so the adapter complacently says:—

"In this old play, what's new we have expressed
In rhyming verse, distinguished from the rest;
That, as the Rhone its hasty way does take,
Not mingling waters, through Geneva's lake,
So, having here the different styles in view,
You may compare the former with the new."

Nor was this merely the insolence of a painter who wipes out the work of an older artist before he begins his own. Samuel Butler, the author of *Hudibras*, positively re-wrote some of his own most characteristic pieces, which had been composed in the older prosody, to conform them to the taste which he had acquired. The difference between the terse and crisp versification of his original *Elephant in the Moon*, did not enable him to prefer it to his later version into what was called "long verse," although the alteration chiefly consisted in the introduction of needless adjectives.

This preference of the new form and complacency in its use grew year by year. We may trace it in the prologues and prefatory dissertations which it became more and more the fashion to prefix to poetry. We find it strongly marked in the initial attempts at versified literary criticism, the *Essay on Poetry* by the Earl of Mulgrave, and the verse-pamphlets of the Earl of Roscommon, although the latter had a certain penchant for smooth blank verse, and was the earliest of the myriad imitators of Milton. But this spirit of self-gratulation reached its pitch when the death of the leaders of the movement, at a great age and almost simultaneously, drew the attention of the critics to what they had performed. Lest I should be supposed to exaggerate or to misrepresent the tone of the age, I will quote from the remarkable preface, unsigned, but written, I believe, by Francis Atterbury, afterwards the famous Bishop of Rochester, for the first edition of Waller's *Posthumous Poems* in 1690[1]. It will be

---

[1] "The Second Part of Mr Waller's Poems, containing his Alteration of the Maid's Tragedy. Together with some other

observed that the writer uses the epithet "Augustan" for the new school of poetry; and this is, I believe, the original occurrence of that phrase; at least, I have met with none earlier:—

"Mr Waller was indeed the parent of English verse, and the first that showed us our tongue had numbers and beauty in it."

This calmly disposes of Spenser and Shakespeare.

"Our language owes more to him than the French does to Cardinal Richelieu, and the whole Academy....The tongue came into his hands like a rough diamond; he polished it first, and to that degree that all artists since him have admired the workmanship, without pretending to mend it....He undoubtedly stands first in the list of refiners, and, for aught I know, last too; for I question whether, in Charles II.'s reign, English did not come to its full perfection, and whether it has not *had* its Augustan age, as well as the Latin; but posterity will best judge of this."

The critic proceeds to examine the language of Waller, and then we come upon this very notable passage upon his versification :—

poems...never put into the first Collection of his Poems. London. Printed for Tho. Bennet, MDCXC." The little volume was licensed Sept. 26, 1689.

"We are no less beholden to Mr Waller for the new turn of verse which he brought in, and the improvement he made in our numbers. Before his time men rimed indeed, and that was all : as for the harmony of measure, and that dance of words, which good ears are so much pleas'd with, they knew nothing of it. Their poetry was then made up almost entirely of monosyllables, which, when they come together in any cluster, are certainly the most harsh untuneable things in the world. If any man doubts of this, let him read ten lines in Donne, and he'll quickly be convinced. Besides their verses ran all into one another, and hung together, throughout a whole copy, like the hooked atoms that compose a body in Descartes.

"There was no distinction of parts, no regular stops, nothing for the ear to rest upon. But as soon as the copy began, down it went, like a larum, incessantly ; and the reader was sure to be out of breath, before he got to the end of it. So that really verse in those days was but down-right prose, tagged with rimes. Mr Waller remov'd all these faults, brought in more polysyllables, and smoother measures ; bound up his thoughts better, and in a cadence more agreeable to the nature of the verse he wrote in ; so that where-ever the natural stops of that were, he contriv'd the little breakings of his sense so as to fall in with 'em. And for that reason, since the stress of our Verse lies commonly upon the last syllable, you'll hardly ever find him using a word of no force there. I would say it if I were not afraid the reader would think me too nice, that he commonly closes with verbs, in which we know the life of language consists[1]."

I have allowed the forgotten and anonymous critic of 1690 to speak thus at length because his language is direct and perspicuous, and because he shows himself here and elsewhere, throughout his discourse, an admirable spokesman for his contemporaries. It cannot but be interesting for us to observe how the whirligig of taste brings in its revenges, and to see how quietly and positively Atterbury condemns those very things which have now come to be again considered beauties, the irregularity of structure in a poem, the use of short Saxon words, the rhythm running down like an alarum. He grasps, too, so very firmly the central notion of the new prosody, its grace, intelligibility, and flexibility, that he leads me easily to the next point that I have to consider with you, namely, what excuse there was for the zeal and satisfaction with which the age accepted the bondage which Waller imposed upon poetry?

[1] See Appendix IV. for the remainder of this preface.

The reaction has now lasted so long and has become so complete, that it is very hard for us to give a just reply to this question. We have been taught, our fathers before us were taught, to loathe the Augustan distich. Among the greatest English poets the one which is most neglected, by far, is Dryden, and mainly because of our prejudice against his couplets. Pope has lately come again more into favour, but it is all that the attraction of his wit can do to drag the ordinary reader over the barrier of his verse. From 1660 onwards to about 1760 the exact opposite was the case. A poet of decent abilities was sure of readers if he would write in the couplet[1]; he had to conquer them if he presumed to stray from it. Like Settle, in Dryden's satire, the poets

"fagotted their fancies as they fell,
And if they rimed and rattled, all was well."

That monstrous play, the *Empress of Marocco*, succeeded in 1673 solely because, in spite of its ineptitudes, the young gentlemen of Cambridge were delighted with the smoothness of the couplets[2]

---

[1] Milton would stand absolutely alone in his preference of another form, if Roscommon also, in 1684, in emulation of *Paradise Lost*, had not chosen to throw off what he calls "the constraint of Rime" in his *Art of Poetry*.

[2] The glibness of Elkanah Settle's verse was certainly remark-

in which it was written. For in the first ardour for the form, its admirers had gone so far as to introduce it into the drama itself, and through some fourteen years rimed plays were the fashion in England. Into this question of the history of dramatic rime I will not, however, enter here, because I regard it as but an episode in the general change of prosody, and also because, in my volume of *Seventeenth Century Studies*, in the chapter dedicated to Sir George Etheredge, I have already given it minute consideration. Here I need refer to it solely as giving us further evidence of the overwhelming partiality of the reading public for what the critic I just now quoted calls, in another place, "true and even riming." Was

able. His early plays trip on their foolish course with a smoothness that must have enraged Dryden. This is the sort of thing :—

"This is no news to that which she has done,
  She was distracted ere the masque begun;
  Alone I saw her in a posture set,
  As if she thought of something high and great;
  Straight with a more than common rage enflamed,
  She moved, stared, walked, stormed, raged, cursed, raved and
     damned;
  With a distorted look she tore her hair,
  Unsheathed her dagger, and gave wounds to air;
  Her face discoloured grew to a deep red,
  As if her looks presaged the blood she shed;
  Then with an infant rage, more soft, more mild,
  She played with madness, leaped, sung, danced and smiled."
                                    Empress of Marocco, IV., 3.

there any excuse, I ask, for a taste so entirely foreign to our own at present?

There would, I think, have been no excuse if the great manner of writing in Elizabeth's reign had been sustained, or if—I will venture to state my paradox boldly—if the great writers had been educated at all points up to the pitch of their genius. But it was not so. It seems to me that the sudden efflorescence of poetry at the close of the sixteenth century came too soon, into a language and a literature still too crude, to be supported. There was, certainly, no depth of cultivation, no broad and wide literary civilization, in the age of Elizabeth. We have a few giants and demigods, we have Shakespeare, Spenser, Bacon, and Jonson; but their manner of writing is peculiar to each, strongly individual, and raised high above the average of their age. I may, perhaps, explain what I mean when I say that if we could totally exclude these authors from our memories, and regard the age without them, it would seem, with certain fragmentary exceptions, more or less an age of barbaric literature. These giants, with the great men who walked beside them, passed away, and left English style strangely unaffected by the glories of their genius. The mediocrities of the age of Charles I. did not model their prose on Bacon or their verse on Shakespeare. They imitated bad Spanish and

Italian types, and wrote as if these great men had never existed.

The romantic writing of the middle of the century is not only weak, it is flaccid, crude, and vicious. A tragic drama printed forty years after the publication of *Cymbeline* reads like the undigested stuff out of which such a perfect growth as Shakespeare's might proceed, not like the product of a stock exhausted by genius. It was this uncultured and barbaric basis to the national literature which made the reformers so anxious for a new order of writing. Not romantic in temper, not ready to be fired by enthusiasm, we do not find the critics of the Restoration warmly praising the masterpieces of the greatest poets. They keep their approbation for such writers as Fairfax, with his Italian sweetness, for Sandys and Randolph, who foresaw the strong plain verse that was about to become fashionable, and they speak of these poets as of forerunners of their own.

The excuse of the classic writers was that they opened a better field for poetry. They would no longer abandon it to the expression of the passions, to a violent ecstasy of feeling; they chained it down to civic uses, made it the vehicle of politics, of morals, of history, of all the fleeting interests of the moment. They brought it up from its country seclusion, and gave it a gay house in Soho Square. I possess, in my own library, a poem which has never been printed, by the famous Lady Winchelsea, in which—the poem was written about 1690—she describes Apollo as presiding at a conference of the Muses :—

"As now he was going to make an oration
  He threw by one lock, with a delicate fashion,
  Upon the left foot most genteely did stand,
  Had drawn back the other, and waved his white hand."

That seems to me to describe the Song-God of the Restoration with the utmost exactitude, a graceful deity, as proud as Sir Fopling Flutter himself of his white hand, and "amber-dropping hair," and postures of a dancing-master. This was a Phœbus[1] whose oration anybody could understand, who would be the patron of vigorous verses if they were also elegant and polite, who would tolerate nothing but common-sense, who did not wish his votaries to sing like birds or waters, but like the chorus in the opera.

The aim was now no longer the expression of passion or fancy; this had been followed to excess,

---

[1] In some sort Waller was this Apollo. Lord Lansdowne (George "Granville, the polite") says, in 1688,
  "The Father of so many gods is he,
   He must himself be sure some deity,
   Minerva and Apollo shall submit,
   And Waller be the only God of Wit."

with the result of a miserable licence of style. A new thing now should be attempted, and poetry should be set to work steadily on the foundations of literature. Many changes had come with the political crisis in the reign of Charles I. Knowledge had increased, curiosity had become more keenly excited, gnomic questions,—questions of theology and morals,—had taken the place in men's minds which had previously been held by mere chivalrous fancies. With all this, a great intellectual weariness settled upon the race, upon all the races of Europe. As the last waves of the Renaissance died away, a deathly calm settled down upon the pools of thought. Man returned from the particular to the general, from romantic examples to those disquisitions on the norm which were thought to display a classical taste. Exhaustion, preference of the form to the matter, craving for a higher standard of elegance in general literature, these were the most prominent of the impulses which led to the wide adoption of the new system of writing. What that system was has been very happily summed up by that admirable critic whom we have just lost, one of the broadest students of poetry that we have ever possessed, the late Rector of Lincoln College. Mark Pattison says: "To give clearness and plainness to the language, to file and finish the lines, to reject superfluity, to diffuse a subdued colour over the whole, to regulate the just subordination of the parts,—these became the business of the poet, and every writer who aspired to be read was a poet."

In other words, the seer disappeared, and the artificer took his place. For a whole century the singer that only sang because he must, and as the linnets do, was entirely absent from English literature. He came back at the close of the eighteenth century with Burns in Scotland and with Blake in England. The lyrical gift, which had overpowered every other through the second quarter of the century, gradually expired, lasting longer, indeed, than we are generally inclined to suppose, but disappearing before the century was out. Dryden's songs, which have been unduly neglected, give us the highest lyrical water-mark of the age. "Farewell, ungrateful traitor," in the *Spanish Fryer*, and the song in *Cleomenes*, are examples of very fine poetry of this species; the latter, which is one of the jewels of the new classical literature, I will now quote, with almost an assurance that it will be new to most of my readers, since no compiler of anthologies has ever searched the tragedies of Dryden for gems, and even the editors of his poetical works have usually omitted his songs.

"No, no, poor suffering heart, no change endeavour!
Choose to sustain the smart, rather than leave her;
My ravished eyes behold such charms about her,
I can die with her, but not live without her;
One tender sigh of hers to see me languish,
Will more than pay the price of my past anguish,
Beware, oh cruel fair, how you smile on me,
'Twas a kind look of yours that has undone me.

"Love has in store for me one happy minute,
And she will end my pain, that did begin it;
Then no day void of bliss, or pleasure, leaving,
Ages shall slide away without perceiving;
Cupid shall guard the door, the more to please us,
And keep out Time and Death, when they would seize us,
Till Time and Death depart, and say, in flying,
Love has found out a way to live by dying."

Here Dryden adopts that very falsetto key of passion which had been habitual with the love-poets of the earlier age. It is therefore a crucial test to apply to this poem the formula of **Mark Pattison**. It endures it with success; it **belongs**, in spite of its theme and temper, essentially to **the new system**. The execution is uniform, the **verse** is not heightened to a pitch at one point, **and** allowed to run down like an alarum at another.

There is an equable force, a general smoothness of expression, all through the song. Then the diction is in every respect other than what Lovelace or Herrick would have made it. It is without local colour, it bears none of the conventional ornaments, "gold," or "roses," "amorous nightingales," and "fresh-quilted colours of Aurora," without which a Marinist poet could hardly venture to address a woman. It has no unusual words, no far-fetched conceits, no superfluous turns of thought, but—considering the tension and extravagance of the feeling described—accomplishes its purpose with the utmost simplicity and common-sense.

It was thoroughly consistent with this desire for smoothness and gentility, that the English writers of the new school should look to France and to French literature, where sentiment and elegance had so long been made the subjects of deliberate study. I have, I hope, shown in earlier lectures that the movement in this direction was begun in England before there was any opportunity for influence from France, and that it was the result of an instinct for form and grace, for intellectual repose, which affected all the races of the west of Europe simultaneously.

But I should be sorry to seem to underrate the part taken by France in the development of

English classicism. The exiles who returned at the Restoration brought back with them the sentimental jargon of the heroic novelists, the *Phébus* as it was called, and this eclectic mode of talking, this simpering style, exercised an overweening influence on polite speech in English. I think that if we ourselves had not forgotten this language, and if the English imitations of it were not more familiar to us than the original, we should be amazed at its effect on the style of the Restoration. Its masterpieces were industriously circulated in English translations during the last years of the Commonwealth. In old country-houses we may still come across these enormous folios, the *Clelia* of Mademoiselle de Scudéry, in particular, dedicated to amorous English maidens, in five huge volumes. I remember that when I was myself a child I got hold of a novel of this class called *Polexander*—I suppose a version of the romance by Gomberville—and read its tedious pages day after day as a sort of religious exercise, tilting the elephantine tome against the wall of the garret where I found it, and really having to enter the book, as if it were a little temple, every time I wanted to proceed with it. The ladies of two centuries ago did much the same, no doubt; they wandered at will for weeks at a time through the monstrous provinces of the country of Tenderness, and lodged in the pretty hamlet of Assiduity by the banks of the river of Inclination; or listened, in the translation of Dr Loveday, to the heroical adventures of La Calprenède's Cleopatra.

All the dramatists, from Dryden downwards, borrowed their tragic plots from these French romances, and the easiest way for a Settle or a Banks to provide himself with material for what was called a heroic play, was to turn the pages of these vast and vapid romances. They were not merely good to steal from, but they supplied matter which was sure to be in sympathy with the tastes of the ordinary play-goer, and thus more and more the appeal was made, not to poets or the illuminated class, but to the general public. The heroes of these extraordinary books of Scudéry and her friends were lifted to a ridiculous height of virtue above ordinary men, their love "made summer at the Arctic pole," their honour was like the diamond and would not endure a microscopical flaw, their courage was enough to discompose the elements and daunt the gods themselves. The consequence of this high ideal was that language was obliged to conform to it, and tragedy became that wonderful thing which we find it in Lee and Crowne. Comedy, on the other hand, and satire, being released from this lofty extravagance, became excessively mundane and vulgar in style, without elevation of any kind, and literature, instead of mingling wit and imagination as the Elizabethans had done, divided the one from the other to the great detriment of both. There was, accordingly, instituted, before anyone had perceived the tendency, a distinction between the language of poetry, which was only to be used by gods and queens and stately gentlemen in full-bottomed wigs, and the language of prose, which was free for the use of these gentlemen when they sat down to a pipe before the kitchen fire, and had hung their periwigs on the backs of their chairs.

There was a constant rivalry between these two styles, tragedy holding its chin high in the air, and comedy laughing at it as Butler laughs in his *Cat and Puss at a Caterwauling*. At last, and this marked the final stage of classical development, the difference between these two classes became slowly extinct. Tragedy lowered its pretensions, and descended from its ranting and roaring fustian down to sober speech; comedy abandoned the intolerable roughness and coarseness of its language, and rose to the grace of Congreve, the manly elegance of Farquhar. Dryden had never quite succeeded in attaining this sobriety; his best pieces are marked by inequalities, he leaps too high and sinks too low.

It was William Walsh, himself a very graceful and sedate writer, who first clearly perceived what was needed. He lacked the force to carry it out, but he pointed the way to Pope. As Pope said to Spence, "Walsh used to tell me that there was one way left of excelling; for though we had several great poets, we never had any one great poet who was *correct*, and he desired me to make that my study and aim." Pope took the advice, and reduced this kind of writing to perfection; in no other country of Europe was there an artist so consummate as he, nowhere one in whom the qualities which Waller and Malherbe and Opitz had imposed upon taste were developed with so much delicacy, variety and harmony. Pope completed the change which had been silently progressing almost from the death of Shakespeare. When Pope's career was finished, it was time to desist, and to prepare for another reaction.

Here I must leave the subject, with a feeling that I have scarcely touched it, so wide is it, so burdened with documents, so set about with the pitfalls of human inconsistency. I hope, however, that I have been able to make a few points clear; in particular, that I have been able to show that the classical movement was not, as has been the habit to suppose, a meaningless and stupid decline into dulness, Hyperion wilfully making a satyr of himself, but that it was a reaction of common-sense from barbarism, a return to rule after licence, an act of self-preservation on the part of literature and language. I shall not be convinced that I am in error in this view by being confronted with a few rainbow-coloured passages from the literature that was superseded, or with instances of vulgarity in the literature that took its place. I hold that it was an absolute necessity, if English poetry was to exist, that a period of executive severity and attention to form should succeed the hysterical riot of the Jacobeans.

The classic movement supplied that basis of style, in prose and verse, upon which all more recent literature has been elevated, and if we have chosen to cover it up and forget it, and to return in our poetical architecture to selected models from earlier schools, it is none the less due to the labours of Waller, Dryden, and Pope, that we have solid groundwork on which to support these brilliant fabrics of the imagination.

APPENDICES.

APPENDIX I.

SIDNEY GODOLPHIN AND SANDYS.

THE very first appearance of the new school of poets in print was, so far as I am able to discover, in George Sandys' *Poems*:—

"A Paraphrase upon the Divine Poems. By George Sandys. London. At the Bell in St Paul's Churchyard. MDCXXXVIII. (Licenced Nov. 1637.)"

To this charming little folio, specially sought after by collectors because it contains Henry Lawes' music to the *Psalms*, both Sidney Godolphin and Waller contributed prefatory eulogies, in company with Lord Falkland, Henry King, Carew, Dudley Digges, and others less eminent. Waller, whose Christian name is misprinted *Edward*, appears with the verses "How bold a work attempts that pen," reprinted in all succeeding collections of his work. Sidney Godolphin's long and courtly poem of compliment has great merit, and in consideration of the entire obscurity which has fallen upon this name, an obscurity from which I hope to be the means in some degree of lifting it, I quote a few stanzas:—

"Music, the universal language, sways
 In every mind; the world this power obeys,
 And Nature's self is charmed by well-tun'd lays.

All disproportioned, harsh, disordered cares,
Unequal thoughts, vain hopes and low despairs
Fly the soft breath of these harmonious airs.

Here is that harp, whose charms uncharm'd the breast
Of troubled Saul, and that unquiet guest
With which his passions travail'd, disposses'd.

* * * * * * *

This work had been proportioned to our sight,
Had you but known with some allay to write,
And not preserv'd your author's strength and light.

But you so crush those odours, so dispense
Those rich perfumes, you make them too intense
And such, alas! as too much please our sense.

We fitter are for sorrows than such love;
Josiah falls, and by his fall doth move
Tears from the people, mourning from above.

Judah, in her Josiah's death, doth die;
All springs of grief are opened to supply
Streams to the torrent of this elegy.

Others break forth in everlasting praise,
Having their wish, and wishing they might raise
Some monument of thanks to after-days.

These are the pictures which your happy art
Gives us, and which so well you do impart,
As if these passions sprang in your own heart.

Others translate, but you the beams collect
Of your inspired authors, and reflect
Those heavenly rays with new and strong effect.

> Yet human language only can restore
> What human language had impaired before,
> And when that once is done, can give no more.
>
> Sir, I forbear to add to what is said,
> Lest to your burnished gold I bring my lead,
> And with what is immortal mix the dead."

Sandys, himself, though with an ear imperfectly trained, is found making a direct effort to reform the lax versification of his day. The volume is, in various ways, one of considerable importance in the history of English poetry.

In view of the curious solidarity of the earliest classical English school, it is not uninteresting to find Hobbes, in his *Leviathan*, incidentally mentioning in these terms of respect a man at least a quarter of a century younger than himself:—" Mr Sidney Godolphin, when he lived, was pleased to think my studies something, and otherwise to oblige me with real testimonies of his good opinion, great in themselves, and the greater for the worthiness of his person."

APPENDIX II.

DENHAM'S ESSAY ON TRANSLATED VERSE.

THERE are so few translations which deserve praise, that I scarce ever saw any which deserv'd pardon; those who travel in that kind, being for the most part so unhappy, as to rob others, without enriching themselves, pulling down the same good authors, without raising their own: neither hath any author been more hardly dealt withall, than this our master [Virgil]: and the reason is evident; for, what is most excellent, is most inimitable, and if even the worst authors are yet made worse by their translators, how impossible is it not to do great injury to the best? And therefore I have not the vanity to think my copy equal to the original, nor (consequently) myself altogether guiltless of what I accuse others; but if I can do Virgil less injury than others have done, it will be, in some degree to do him right; and indeed, the hope of doing him more right is the only scope of this Essay, by opening this new way of translating this author, to those whom youth, leisure, and better fortune make fitter for such undertakings.

I conceive it a vulgar error in translating poets, to affect being *fidus interpres;* let that care be with them who deal in matters of fact, or matters of faith: but whosoever aims at it in poetry, as he attempts what is not required, so he shall never perform what he attempts; for it is not his business alone to translate language into language, but poesie into poesie; and poesie is of so subtle a spirit, that in pouring out of one language into another, it will all evaporate; and if a new spirit be not added in the transfusion, there will remain nothing but a *caput mortuum*, there being certain graces and happinesses peculiar to every language, which gives life and energy to the words; and whosoever offers at verbal translation, shall have the misfortune of that young traveller, who lost his own language abroad, and brought home no other instead of it: for the grace of the Latin will be lost by being turned into English words; and the grace of the English, by being turned into the Latin phrase. And as speech is the apparel of our thoughts, so are there certain garbs and modes of speaking, which vary with the times; the fashion of our clothes being not more subject to alteration, than that of our speech: and this I think Tacitus means, by that which he calls *Sermonem temporis istius auribus accommodatum;* the delight of change being as due to the curiosity of the ear, as of the eye; and therefore if Virgil must needs speak English, it were fit he should speak not only as a man of this Nation, but as a man of this Age; and if this disguise I have put upon him (I wish I could give it a better name) sit not naturally and easily on so grave a person, yet it may become him better than that fools-coat, wherein the French and Italian have of late presented him; at least, I hope, it will not make him appear deformed, by making any part enormously bigger or less than the life, (I having made it my principal care to follow him, as he made it his to follow nature in all his proportions). Neither have I anywhere offered such violence to his sense, as to make it seem mine, and not his. Where my expressions are not so full as his, either our language, or my art were defective (but I rather suspect my self); but where mine are fuller than his, they are but the impressions which the often reading of him, hath left upon my thoughts; so that if they are not his own conceptions, they are at least the results of them; and if (being conscious of making him speak worse than he did almost in every line) I err in endeavouring sometimes to make him speak better; I hope it will be judged an error on the right hand, and such an one as may deserve pardon, if not imitation.

APPENDIX III.

Waller's Address to the Queen.

The following address to Queen Henrietta Maria, under a slight concealment, was issued with some copies of the genuine edition of Waller's *Poems* in 1645, but immediately suppressed. It seems to me worthy of revival.

To my Lady.

Madam,

Your commands for the gathering of these sticks into a faggot, had sooner been obeyed, but, intending to present you with my whole vintage, I stayed till the latest grapes were ripe, for here your Ladyship hath not only all I have done, but all I ever mean to do in this kind: not but that I may defend the attempt I have made upon poetry, by the examples (not to trouble you with history) of many wise and worthy persons of our own times, as Sir Philip Sydney, Sir Fra. Bacon, Cardinal Perron, the ablest of his country-men; and the former Pope, who they say, in stead of the triple crown, wore sometimes the poet's ivy, as an ornament, perhaps of lesser weight and trouble, but Madam, these nightingales sung only in the spring, it was the diversion of their youth. As ladies learn to sing and play when they are children, what they forget when they are women; the resemblance holds further: for as you quit the lute the sooner, because the posture is suspected to draw the body awry, so this is not always practised without some villany to the mind, wresting it from present occasions, and accustoming us to a still somewhat removed from common use. But that you may not think his case deplorable, who had made verses, we are told, that Tully (the greatest wit among the Romans) was once sick of this disease, and yet recovered so well; that of almost as bad a poet as your servant, he became the most perfect orator in the world. So that not so much to have made verses, as not to give over in time, leaves a man without excuse: the former presenting us with an opportunity at least of doing wisely: that is to conceal those we have made, which I shall yet do, if my humble request may be of as much force with your Ladyship, as your commands have been with me. Madam, I only whisper these in your ears; if you publish them, they are your own, and therefore as you apprehend the reproach of a wit, and a poet, cast them into the fire, or if they come where green boughs are in the chimney, with the help of your fair friends, (for thus bound, it will be too hard a task for your hands alone) to tear them in pieces, wherein you shall honour me with the fate of Orpheus, for so his poems, whereof we only hear the form (not his limbs as the story will have it) I suppose were scattered by the Thracian dames. Here, Madam, I might take an opportunity to celebrate your virtues, and to instruct you how unhappy you are, in that you know not who you are: how much you excel the most excellent of your own : and how much you amaze the least inclined to wonder of your sex. But as they will be apt to take your Ladyship for a Roman name: so would they believe that I endeavoured the character of a perfect nymph, worshipt an image of my own making, and dedicated this to the Lady of the brain, not of the heart of your Ladyships most humble servant.

E. W.

APPENDIX IV.

The Preface to Waller's Posthumous Poems, 1690.

The Reader need be told no more in commendation of these Poems, than that they are Mr Waller's: A name that carries every thing in it, that's either great or graceful in poetry. He was indeed the parent of English verse, and the first that shew'd us our tongue had beauty and numbers in it. Our language owes more to him than the French to Cardinal Richlieu, and the whole Academy. A poet cannot think of him, without being in the same rapture Lucretius is in, when Epicurus comes in his way :—

> Tu pater et rerum inventor, Tu patria nobis
> Suppeditas præcepta : Tuisque ex inclyte, chartis
> Floriferis ut apes in saltibus omnia libant
> Omnia nos itidem depascimur aurea dicta :
> Aurea, perpetua semper dignissima vita.

The tongue came into his hands, like a rough diamond; he polish'd it first, and to that degree that all artists since him have admired the workmanship, without pretending to mend it. Sucklyn and Carew, I must confess, wrote some few things smoothly enough, but as all they did in this kind was not very considerable, so 'twas a little later than the earliest pieces of Mr Waller. He undoubtedly stands first in the list of refiners, and for ought I know, last too; for I question whether in Charles the Second's reign, English did not come to its full perfection; and whether it has not had its Augustean Age, as well as the Latin. It seems to be already mix'd with foreign languages, as far as its purity will bear; and, as chymists say of their menstruums, to be quite sated with the infusion. But posterity will best judge of this.......In the mean time, 'tis a surprizing reflection, that between what Spenser wrote last, and Waller first, there should not be much above twenty years distance: and yet the one's language, like the money of that time, is as currant now as ever; whilst the other's words are like old coins, one must go to an antiquary to understand their true meaning and value. Such advances may a great genius make, when it undertakes any thing in earnest!

Some painters will hit the chief lines, and master strokes of a face so truly, that through all the differences of age, the picture shall still bear a resemblance. This art was Mr Waller's; he sought out, in this flowing tongue of ours, what parts would last, and be of standing use and ornament; and this he did so successfully, that his language is now as fresh as it was at first setting out. Were we to judge barely by the wording, we could not know what was wrote at twenty, and what at fourscore. He complains indeed of a tide of words that comes in upon the English poet, o'reflows whatever he builds: but this was less his case than any man's, that ever wrote; and the mischief on't is, this very complaint will last long enough to confute it self. For though English be mouldring stone, as he tells us there, yet he has certainly pick'd the best out of a bad quarry.

We are no less beholden to him for the new turn of verse, which he brought in, and the improvement he made in our numbers. Before his time, men rim'd indeed, and that was all: as for the harmony of measure, and that dance of words, which good ears are so much pleas'd with, they knew nothing of it. Their Poetry then was made up almost entirely of monosyllables; which, when they come together in any cluster, are certainly the most harsh untunable things in the world. If any man doubts of this, let him read ten lines in Donne, and he'll be quickly convinc'd. Besides, their verses ran all into one another, and hung together, throughout a whole copy, like the *hook't atoms*, that compose a body in Des Cartes. There was no distinction of parts, no regular stops, nothing for the ear to rest upon.......But as soon as the copy began, down it went like a larum, incessantly; and the reader was sure to be out of breath, before he got to the end of it. So that really verse in those days was but down-right prose, tagg'd with rimes. Mr Waller remov'd all these faults, brought in more polysyllables, and smoother measures; bound up his thoughts better, and in a cadence more agreeable to the nature of the verse he wrote in: so that where-ever the natural stops of that were, he contriv'd the little breakings of his sense so as to fall in with 'em. And for that reason, since the stress of our verse lies commonly upon the last syllable, you'll hardly ever find him using word of no force there. I would say if I were not afraid the reader would think me too nice, that he commonly closes with verbs, in which we know the life of language consists.

Among other improvements, we may reckon that of his rimes. Which are always good, and very often the better for being new. He had a fine ear, and knew how quickly that sense was cloy'd by the same round of chiming words still returning upon it. 'Tis a decided case by the great master of writing. Quæ sunt ampla et pulchra, diu placere possunt; quæ lepida et concinna, (amongst which rhyme must, whether it will or no, take its place) *cito satietate afficiunt aurium sensum fastidiosissimum.* This he understood very well, and therefore, to take off the danger of a surfeit that way, strove to please by variety, and new sounds. Had he carried this observation (among others) as far as it would go, it must, methinks, have shown him the incurable fault of this jingling kind of poetry, and have led his later judgment to blank verse. But he continu'd an obstinate lover of rime to the very last. 'Twas a mistress, that never appear'd unhandsome in his eyes, and was courted by him long after Sacharissa was forsaken. He had rais'd it, and brought it to that perfection we now enjoy it in: and the Poet's temper (which has always a little vanity in it) would not suffer him ever to slight a thing, he had taken so much pains to adorn. My Lord Roscommon was more impartial: no man ever rim'd truer and evener than he, yet he is so just as to confess, that 'tis but a trifle, and to wish the tyrant dethron'd, and blank verse set up in its room. There is a third person[1], the

---

[1] Dryden.

living glory of our English poetry, who has disclaim'd the use of it upon the stage, tho no man ever employ'd it there so happily as he. 'Twas the strength of his genius that first brought it into credit in plays; and 'tis the force of his example that has thrown it out again. In other kinds of writing it continues still; and will do so, till some excellent spirit arises, that has leisure enough, and resolution to break the charm, and free us from the troublesome bondage of riming.

As Mr Milton very well calls it, and has prov'd it as well, by what he has wrote in another way. But this is a thought for times at some distance; the present age is a little too warlike: it may perhaps furnish out matter for a good poem in the next, but 'twill hardly encourage one now: without prophesying, a man may easily know, what sort of laurels are like to be in request.

Whilst I am talking of verse, I find my self, I don't know how, betray'd into a great deal of prose. I intended no more than to put the reader in mind, what respect was due to any thing that fell from the pen of Mr Waller. I have heard his last printed copies, which are added in the several editions of his poems, very slightly spoken of; but certainly they don't deserve it. They do indeed discover themselves to be his last, and that's the worst we can say of 'em. He is there Jam senior: sed cruda deo viridisque senectus. The same censure perhaps will be passed on the pieces of this second part. I shall not so far engage for 'em, as to pretend they are all equal to whatever he wrote in the vigour of his youth. Yet they are so much of a piece with the rest, that any man will at first sight know 'em to be

Mr Waller's. Some of 'em were wrote very early, but not put in former collections, for reasons obvious enough, but which are now ceas'd. The Play was alter'd, to please the Court. 'Tis not to be doubted who sat for the two brothers characters. 'Twas agreeable to the sweetness of Mr Waller's temper, to soften the rigour of the tragedy, as he expresses it; but whether it be so agreeable to the nature of tragedy it self, to make every thing come off easily, I leave to the critics. In the prologue, and epilogue, there are a few verses that he has made use of upon another occasion. But the reader may be pleased to allow that in him, that has been allowed so long in Homer and Lucretius. Exact writers dress up their thoughts so very well always, that when they have need of the same sense, they can't put it into other words, but it must be to its prejudice. Care has been taken in this book to get together everything of Mr Waller's, that's not put into the former collection; so that between both, the reader may make the set complete.

It will perhaps be contended after all, that some of these ought not to have been publish'd: and Mr Cowley's decision will be urg'd, that a neat tomb of marble is a better monument, than a great pile of rubbish, etc. It might be answer'd to this, that the pictures and poems of great masters have been always valu'd, tho the last hand weren't put to 'em. And I believe none of those gentlemen that will make the objection would refuse a sketch of Raphael's or one of Titian's draughts of the first sitting.

I might tell 'em too, what care has been taken by the

learned, to preserve the fragments of the ancient Greek and Latin poets: There has been thought to be a Divinity in what they said, and therefore the least pieces of it have been kept up and reverenc'd, like religious reliques. And I am sure, take away the *mille anni*, and impartial reasoning will tell us, there is as much due to the memory of Mr Waller, as to the most celebrated names of antiquity.

But to wave the dispute now of what ought to have been done; I can assure the reader, what would have been had this edition been delay'd. The following poems were got abroad, and in a great many hands: It were vain to expect that amongst so many admirers of Mr Waller, they should not meet with one fond enough to publish 'em. They might have staid indeed, till by frequent transcriptions they had been corrupted extreamly, and jumbled together with things of another kind: But then they would have found their way into the world. So 'twas thought a greater piece of kindness to the author, to put 'em out; whilst they continue genuine and unmix'd; and such, as he himself, were he alive might own.

INDEX.

Addison, Joseph, versification of his school of poetry, 55 n.
Adventure, spirit of, its decline after the Elizabethans, 35, 6
Æneid, Thos. Phaer's translation of, 187
Against Love, passage from Denham's, 133, 4
Akenside, Mark, 45
Albion's England, by William Warner, 75
Albovine, by Sir W. Davenant, 146 n., 150, 165 n. 1
Alcippe of François Maynard, its resemblance to Denham's *Cooper's Hill*, 120
"Alexandrian" literature, artificial nature of, 181, 205
Alexandrine verse, little used by Malherbe, 20, 1; how handled by Corneille and in England, 121
Anapaestic cadence, neglected in English verse from Chaucer to Waller, 9, 187, 8
Andrewes, Lancelot, Bp of Winchester, 53
Anne of Austria, her sympathy with Queen Henrietta Maria, 113, 117; French poetry in her time, 119
Annus Mirabilis, one of the few great poems composed in the four-line heroic stanza, 165;

influence of *Gondibert* on its style, 228
Arcadia, its languid and difficult style, 25, 75
Aristotle's rules of composition, 38
Armstrong, John, obscurity of his figures of speech, 12
Arnold, Matthew, his essay on Falkland, 115
Arrebo, first modern Danish poet, 16
Ars Poetica, Horace's warnings in, justified by the extravagance of the early Caroline writings, 37—9
Art of Poetry, by Wentworth Dillon, Earl of Roscommon, 252 n. 1
Astraea Redux, Dryden's style in the, 228
Atterbury, Francis, Bp of Rochester, his criticism of Waller, 248—251
Aubrey, John, 142 n. 2, 144, 167, 236 n.
'Augustan,' the epithet, first applied by Francis Atterbury, 249
Augustan critics, 104
,, distich, 252; its earlier and later character, as shewn in Chamberlayne's *Pharonnida* and Keats' *Endymion*, 201

Ayres, Philip, tries to restore romantic poetry, 210; his sonnets, 211

Bacon, Lord Francis, his writings in advance of his age, 254
Banks, Ann, marries Waller, 60
Barnfield, Richard, 24
Baron, Robert, his tragedy of *Mirza,* and reference to Denham's *Sophy,* 100 n.
Barons' Wars, by Michael Drayton, 34, 5, 75
Bartholomew Fair, by Ben Jonson, resembles the works of the Dutch dramatist, Brederô, 17 n.
Battle of the Summer Islands, by Ed. Waller, 65, 73—6; imitated in Davenant's *Madagascar,* 150
Beaumont, Joseph, his *Psyche,* 172
Behn, Aphara, her eulogy on Waller, 182 n.
Bermuda Islands, the scene of Waller's *Battle of the Summer Islands,* 73, 4 n.
Bermudas, The, of Andrew Marvell, 220
Betterton, Thos., the actor, 144
Biographia Britannica, its opinion of Waller in 1766, 45; reference to Denham in, 243 n. 2
Blake, Wm., his place in English poetry corresponds with that of Burns in Scotch, 258
Boileau, Nicholas, 20
Botticelli, 30
Boyle, Roger, see Lord Orrery
Brederô, the greatest Dutch dramatist, 17 n.
Britannia's Pastorals, by Wm. Browne, 104
Brooke, Lord, Fulke Greville, his patronage of and influence upon Wm. Davenant, 145—8 151, 166
Browne, Wm., 104, 137
Buckingham, (First) Duke of, George Villiers, reception of the news of his death by Charles I., and Waller's verses on the occasion, 61, 2
   „   (Second) Duke of, George Villiers, 245
Burne-Jones, Edward, his painting compared to Thomas Stanley's poetry, 206
Burns, Robert, as the reviver of romantic poetry in Scotland, corresponds to Blake in England, 258
Butler, Samuel, his *Hudibras,* 116, 184, 186; conforms to the classical style, 247, 8; ridicules the vapid and highflown style of tragedy borrowed from France, 263
Byron, Lord, in his Greek romances a successor of Wm. Chamberlayne, 200

Calamy, Dr Edmund, extract from Wild's poem on his death, 193 n.
Cambridge, a 'hotbed of poetry' in the early Caroline period, 24, 5, 37; Waller a scholar at King's, 51; relics of Gray at Pembroke, 165; Cowley, a precocious Cambridge verseman, 172; the Marinist school there, 172; Cleveland sows his poetical wild oats there, 185, 190; Robert Wild's picture of life there under the Commonwealth, 194—6; Thomas Stanley at Pembroke, 204; Henry Vaughan, the Silurist, the last survivor of

Herbert's school there, 209; Andrew Marvell, kidnapped from Trinity by the Jesuits, 212, 3; popularity of Settle's *Empress of Marocco* at, 252

Campbell, Thomas, one of the first of the critics to resuscitate Chamberlayne's *Pharonnida*, 200

Campion, Thomas, his tumbling, rimeless measure, 9 n.

Carew, Thomas, 22, 27, 38, 82 n., 150, 208

Chace, The, passage from Somerville's, 108 n. 2

"Chalkhill, John," the pseudonym under which Izaak Walton published *Thealma and Clearchus*, 209 n. 2

Chamberlayne, William, 197—203; Keats' indebtedness to him, 199; his Greek romance *Pharonnida* a forerunner of Byron's writings, 200

Chapelain, Jean, relation of his writings to Cowley's, 119

Chapman, George, 24, 56, 75

Charles I., discourages the writing of poetry, 22; Waller's poem on his escape from shipwreck at Santander, 56—8; fosters by his stupidity the new mental and political ideas of his time, 33; his reception of the news of Buckingham's death, 61, 2; referred to in Waller's poem on the rebuilding of St Paul's, 80, 1; his treatment of Waller at Oxford, 85; warning reference to him in Denham's *Sophy*, 102, 3; his qualified praise of *Cooper's Hill*, and unsympathetic advice to Denham, 130, 1

Charles II., 113, 116, 131, 232, 235

Charles' Spikenard, by John Cleveland, 186

Chatterton, Thomas, an opponent of the classical school, 4

Chetwood, Knightly, Dean of Gloucester, his criticism of English poetry, 32 n. 2

Chiabrera, his position in Italy analogous to our Cowley, 15

Chloris and Hilas, by Waller, one of the earliest dactylic poems, 188

Christ's Victory and Triumph, by Giles Fletcher, 75

Cid, Corneille's, 101

Cinna, Corneille's, 102

Claremont, by Samuel Garth, a direct imitation of *Cooper's Hill*, 108

Clarendon, Edward Hyde, Earl of, 60, 61, 63, 83, 86 and n. 1, 90, 115, 123, 146 n., 237

Classical reaction, the mental condition which rendered it possible, 35—9

Classical school, the language and peculiarities of, 10—13, 169; Denham's *Sophy* its first published representative, 95, 6; its triumph in *Cooper's Hill*, 103, 4; not due to French influence, 111, 12; the final stage of its development, 263

Classicism in Dutch literature, 18

Cleland, William, 194 n.

Cleopatra, of Samuel Daniel, 102 n.

Cleveland, John, released by Oliver Cromwell, 116, 7; has secured no place in the history of English poetry, 184; at first a Marinist, 185; his undergraduate days at Cambridge, 185, 190; a disappointment in both politics and poetry,

186; his use of the triple cadence in lyrics, 187—90

Cockaine, Sir Aston, might have been the Boswell of the early Caroline period, 24

Coleridge, Samuel Taylor, assists to revolutionize the taste for classical poetry, 4, 178; his triumph foreseen by Southey, 156; his criticism of Donne, 217; the self-reserve necessary in reading some of his poems, 217

Congreve, William, his refining influence upon Comedy, 263

Contarini, 61

Cooper's Hill, Denham's praise of Waller in his poem of, 79, 80; Dryden's opinion of, 95; date of its publication, 96, 103; a decisive victory for the classical school, 104; its place among topographical poems, 104; subsequent alterations of the first edition, 105—7; reasons for the poem's great and enduring reputation, 107—9; imitated in Pope's *Windsor Forest* and Garth's *Claremont*, 108; its resemblance to Maynard's *Alcippe*, 120; its influence on Herrick, 246

Corbet, Richard, Bishop of Norwich, 187

Corneille, Pierre, doubtful whether he had any influence upon Denham's writings, 101, 2; brings the Alexandrine verse to perfection, 121

Coronation Panegyric, of John Dryden, 228

Cowley, Abraham, 135—78 passim; his position analogous to that of Chiabrera in Italy, 15, 19, 108; attached to Queen Henrietta Maria during the Exile, 113; meets Crashaw in poverty in Paris, 114, 118; French influence upon him, 119, 121; his desertion from the romantic to the classical school, 140; his place among the classicists, 171, 177; his undergraduate life at Cambridge, 172; comparison between him and Victor Hugo, 173; passage from his *Elegy* on Crashaw, 173—175; his *Davideis*, 175, 6; Pope's sneer at him, 177 and n.; revival of his influence, 177, 8; Denham's last verses written for his funeral, 244

Crabbe, George, his effect on the fame of classical poetry, 4

Crashaw, Richard, style of his *Weeping of the Magdalen*, 14 n.; starving in Paris during the Exile, 114; character of his verse while at Cambridge, 172 and n.; passage from Cowley's *Elegy* on him, 173—175

Crawley, Sir Francis, Judge, impeached by Waller on the ship-money question, 84

Cromwell, Oliver, related to Edmund Waller, 49, 83; releases John Cleveland from prison at Yarmouth, 117; Mrs Waller makes capital of her relationship with him, but is eventually silenced, 122, 229; Marvell's Horatian ode on him, 216; Waller's *Panegyric* to him, 129, 30, 231, 2

Crowne, John, dramatist, 262

Cruel Brother, by William Davenant, 147

Cupid Crucified, by Thomas Stanley, 206, 7

Curse of Kehama, by Robert Southey, 158

Cyder, of John Philips, its pompous diction, 11 n.

Dactylic movement unknown to the Elizabethans, 9, 10, 187; introduced by Waller and Cleveland, 188, 9

Daniel, Samuel, his tragi-comedies *Cleopatra* and *Philotas*, 102 n.

Darwin, Erasmus, pomposity of his figures of speech, 12, 170

Daubigny, Lady, shares in the plot of 1643 against the Parliament, 86

Davenant, Sir William, 135—78 passim; 108, 113, 118, 121; a pervert from the romantic school, 140; the legendary son of Shakespeare, 144, 5; his friendship with Fulke Greville, Lord Brooke, 145—8; in 1637 succeeds Ben Jonson as poet laureate, 149; his place among the renovators of English verse, 152, 3; compared with Southey, 155—9; his life saved by Milton's interposition, 167

Davideis, a sacred epic by Abraham Cowley, 173, 175; passage quoted from, 176

Davies, Sir John, one of the first to employ the four-line heroic stanza, 165

Dekker, Thomas, dramatist, 17

Denham, Sir John, not affected by French classicism, 21; Waller's earliest pupil in poetry, 63; his criticism of Waller, 79, 80; Dryden's opinion of his *Cooper's Hill*, 95; his *Sophy* the first publication of the classical school, 95, 6, 99—103; his youth, 96, 7; his *Essay against Gaming*, 97, 8; his *Destruction of Troy*, 98; was he influenced by Corneille? 101, 2; his *Cooper's Hill*, 103—9, 121; Charles I.'s unsympathetic advice to him, 131; describes the life of the cavaliers during the Exile, 114 n.; 118; his career during the Commonwealth, 130—3; passage from his poem *Against Love*, 133, 4; his essay on the art of translating, 98, 9, 272—4

Destruction of Troy, by Sir John Denham, 98

D'Ewes, Sir Symeon, 87; extract from his diary describing Waller's appearance at the bar of the House of Commons, 89 n.

Dido and Æneas, by Sir Richard Fanshawe, 118

Digby, Lord George, an opponent of the 'Root and Branch' party, 84

Digges, Sir Dudley, 269

Diodati, Dr John, visited at Geneva by Waller, 128

Divine Love, by Waller, passage from, 240, 1

Dobson, Austin, his suggestion of an English term for the French *enjambement*, 6

Donne, John, a leader in literature, 14, 182; has a literary acquaintance with Constantine Huyghens, 17; popularity of his poems at Cambridge, 25 and n. 1, 37; 67, 121, 151 n.; Marvell the last of his school, 216; Coleridge's criticism of him, 217; passage from his *Valediction forbidding Mourning*, 217; Francis Atterbury's opinion of his verse, 250

Dramatists of the early Caroline period prepare the way for the prosaic reaction, 29
,, French, their influence upon England, 262
Drayton, Michael, his *Barons' Wars*, 34, 5, 75; 56, 67; his *Polyolbion*, 104
Dryden, John, class of poetry identified with, 3; effect of the naturalistic poets on his fame, 4; specimen of his verse from *Mac-Flecknoe*, 7; Waller's verse compared with his, 20, 58, 210, 233; at one time reckoned inferior to Waller, 48 n.; his opinion of Waller's verse, 54, 5, 95, 153; his *Hind and the Panther*, 75; his opinion of Denham's *Cooper's Hill*, 95; his treatment of the Alexandrine, 121, 234, 5; in the first rank of seventeenth century writers, 137; employs in his *Annus Mirabilis* the four-line heroic stanza, 165, 228; Cowley's influence upon him, 177, 227; influence of Cleveland's satires on his style, 192 n. 1; a friend of Philip Ayres, 211; had no share in the early development of the classical movement, 226—8; at first a Marinist, 227; influence of Davenant's *Gondibert* seen in his *Heroic Stanzas* and *Annus Mirabilis*, 228; Oldham's influence upon his satires, 234 and n.; reason for the present neglect of his writings, 252; his opinion of Elkanah Settle's verse, 252 and n. 2; character of his songs, 258—60; his dramas, 263; a pillar of classical poetry, 265

Duchess of Malfy, by John Webster, 24
Dunciad, by Alexander Pope, 75
Dutch poetry during the seventeenth century, 17, 8
Dyer, Sir Edward, a friend of Lord Brooke and Sir Philip Sidney, 145

Elegy in a Country Churchyard, use of the four-line heroic stanza by Thomas Gray in his, 164—6
Elephant in the Moon, by Samuel Butler, 248
Elizabethan poetry, its spirit and characteristics, 13, 33, 35, 6, 75
Ellice, Robert, 165 n. 1
Empress of Marocco, passage from Elkanah Settle's, 252 n. 2
Endymion, by John Keats, its connexion with William Chamberlayne's *Pharonnida*, 199, 200, 201
Enjambement, specimen of the French, 6; English term of 'overflow' proposed for it, 6, 55
Entertainment at Rutland House, by Sir William Davenant, 168
Essay against Gaming, by Sir John Denham, 97, 99
Eusden, Lawrence, 228
Evelyn, John, travels with Waller during the Exile, 125—8; thinks Sir John Denham "a better poet than architect," 242 n.

Faery Queen, of Edmund Spenser, 26, 247
Fairfax, Edward, 255
Faithful Shepherdess, by John Fletcher, 38

Falconer, William, 45
Falkland, Viscount, Lucius Cary, Waller a member of his club, 62; an opponent of the 'Root and Branch' party, 84; falls at the (first) battle of Newbury, 114; Clarendon's opinion of him, 115
Fanshawe, Sir Richard, in 1646 carries the Prince of Wales (Charles II.) safely to Paris, 116; not influenced by French literature during the Exile, 118; a full-blown Marinist, 118, 9; 121; his *Pastor Fido*, 118, 131
Farquhar, George, his refining influence upon Comedy, 263
Fenton, Elijah, lines on Waller's Sacharissa, 64 n. 1; editor of Waller's poems, 110, 125
Ferrarius, Dr Franciscus, visited by Waller and Evelyn at Milan, 126
Filicaja, reference to his effect on Italian poetry, 15
Flatman, Thomas, 209 n. 2
Fletcher, John, dramatist, his *Faithful Shepherdess*, 38, 100, 137
Fletcher, Phineas, 22; his *Purple Island*, 26, 27, 34, 38, 159
Fletcher, Giles (brother of Phineas F.), 75
Ford, John, dramatist, 24, 100
France, had very little share in originating the classical movement in England, 18—21, 111, 112, 260; but influenced its development very considerably, 112, 119, 120, 260, 261; connexion of its drama with that of England, 100—102, 262; its literature at the time of the Exile, 119—122

Fuscara, passage from John Cleveland's, 185 n.

Garden, The, by Andrew Marvell, 219, 220
Gardiner, Prof. S. R., 86 n. 2, 88 n., 123
Gargantua, by Rabelais, referred to, 46 and n.
Garth, Sir Samuel, imitates *Cooper's Hill* in his *Claremont*, 108
German poetry, beginning of modern, 16
Godolphin, Sidney, unaffected by the French classical revolt, 21; killed in the Civil War, 109; passages from his writings, 110, 269; his skill in the treatment of the couplet, 111, 116; a friend of Lord Falkland, 115; his poem to G. Sandys, 269, 270; Hobbes' mention of him in his *Leviathan*, 271
Gondibert, by Sir William Davenant, 139; its important place in the history of the classical transition, 146, 155, 158, 159; time of its publication, 153—5; allusions to it in contemporary literature, 159—162; plot of the poem, 162; passage quoted from it, 163; its metre, 164—6; its effect on Dryden, 228
Gongora, Luis, Spanish poet, 13, 22
Granville, George, Lord Lansdowne, his estimate of Waller, 256 n.
Gray, Thomas, opposed to the classical school of verse, 4, 50; his use of the four-line heroic stanza, 164—6; revives Cowley's prosody, 177
Greene, Robert, 23

Greville, Fulke, see Brooke, Lord

Habington, William, 22, 150, 208
Halifax, Lord, George Savile, a pupil of Waller's in verse, 236
Hallo my Fancy, by William Cleland, 194 n.
Hammond, James, his *Love Elegies*, 165, 166
Hampden, John, his sister the mother of Edmund Waller, 49, 122; 83, 84
Hardy, Alexandre, French dramatist, 101
Harvey, Gabriel, 24
Hausted, Peter, 116
Henrietta Maria, Queen of Charles I., attended in her exile by men of letters, 113; well received in France, 117, 121; marries Lord Jermyn after Charles I.'s death, 122
Herbert, George, 22, 38, 209
,, Sir William, 100 n. 1
Heroic Stanzas, by John Dryden, 228
Herrick, Robert, 22, 48 n., 137, 260; momentary influence upon him of *Cooper's Hill*, 246
Heywood, Thomas, dramatist, 24
Hind and the Panther, by John Dryden, 75
Hobbes, Thomas, his rule for the composition of an heroic poem, 75; in Paris during the Exile, 113, 118; replies to Davenant's preface to *Gondibert*, 154; his translation of Homer, 165 and n. 2; his criticism of Sidney Godolphin, 271
Holiday, Barton, 123
Holland, character of its literature during the seventeenth century, 17, 18
Homer, Thomas Hobbes' translation of, 165 and n. 2
Hope, Anastatius, 200
Horace, his style described by Waller, 3; his warnings in the *Ars Poetica* justified by the grotesqueness of the early Caroline writers, 38
Hudibras, by Samuel Butler, 116, 184, 186, 247
Hugo, Victor, in some points resembles Cowley, 173
Huyghens, Constantine, a literary friend of John Donne, 17

Iliad, Thomas Hobbes' translation of the, 165 n. 2
Italy, condition of poetry at close of the sixteenth century, 14, 15
Iter Boreale, by Robert Wild, 161, 191, 192, 197

Jermyn, Henry, Lord, marries Queen Henrietta Maria, 122; introduces Davenant to her notice, 149
Jodelle, Étienne, French dramatist, 102 n.
Johnson, Samuel, class of poetry identified with, 3; his criticism of Denham, 108 n. 1; 216
Jones, Inigo, 242, 243
Jonson, Ben, resemblance of his works to those of the Dutch Brederô, 17 and n.; 24, 56, 58, 62, 137, 254; place of his *Penshurst* among topographical poems, 104

Keats, John, quotation from his *Sleep and Poetry* on the preceding period of classical poetry, 4, 5; the passage a

specimen of the romantic order, 7, 199; his contrast to Dryden, 7; his generation not qualified as critics of classical poetry, 9; indebted in *Endymion* to Chamberlayne's *Pharonnida*, 199; his treatment of the heroic couplet, 199, 200
Killigrew, Thomas, 114 and n.
King, Henry (Bishop of Chichester), 269

Lalla Rookh, by Thomas Moore, 189
Lamartine, Alphonse, 83
Lamb, Charles, his admiration of Cyril Tourneur's plays, 31
Landor, Walter Savage, his estimate of Southey as a poet, 157
Lansdowne, Lord, George Granville, his estimate of Waller, 256 n.
Last Instructions to a Painter, by Andrew Marvell, 243 n. 1
Lee, Nathaniel, dramatist, 262
Levite's Revenge, by Robert Gomershall, 34
Lodge, Thomas, 23, 24, 36
Love Elegies, by James Hammond, 165
Love's Victory, by William Chamberlayne, 198
Lovelace, Richard, 27, 208, 260
Lower, Sir William, 171
Lucas, Margaret, Duchess of Newcastle, 113
Lyly, John, reference to, 13

Macaulay, Lord, 25
Mac-Flecknoe, passage from Dryden's, 7
Madagascar, by William Davenant, 139, 149 n., 150, 151
Maid's Tragedy, by Beaumont and Fletcher, originally in blank verse, re-written in rimed couplets by Waller, 247
Malherbe, François de, the first to introduce polish and correctness into poetry, 19, 20, 21, 69 n., 119, 120, 264
Marini, Gianbattista, referred to, 13, 22, 24, 40, 118, 121, 150, 216; folly of his school, 15, 27, 172, 210, 260
Marius the Epicurean, by Walter Pater, 207 n.
Mark Anthony, by John Cleveland, an example of the early use of the triple cadence, 189
Marlowe, Christopher, 17
Marvell, Andrew, 137, 243 n. 1; a pupil of Cleveland in satire, 192; sketch of his life and work, 211—221
Mason, John, 28
Massinger, Philip, 24, 100
May, Thomas, tragic poet, 91
Maynard, François, pupil of Malherbe, his *Alcippe* compared with *Cooper's Hill*, 120
Menteur, Le, by Pierre Corneille, 121
'Metaphysical,' the name given by Dr Johnson to the Marinists, 23, 27, 216
Middleton, Thomas, 24
Milton, John, his description of metrical 'enjambement,' 6 n.; his relation to the Dutch poet Vondel, 17; at first a Marinist, as in his *Nativity Ode*, 40, 172; his retirement to Horton, 40, 41, 50, 139; at one time reckoned inferior to Waller, 48 and n.; his lyrics imitated in Robert Baron's *Mirza*, 100 n.; 125, 137, 140; pleads successfully with Cromwell for Davenant's life, a service which Davenant

repaid at the Restoration, 167, 170; at Cambridge, 172, 175, 228; his preference for blank verse, 248, 252 n. 1

Mirza, by Robert Baron, 100 n. 1

Monk, George (Duke of Albemarle), 192 and n. 2

Montchrestien, Antoine, 101

Moore, Thomas, 74 n., 189

More, Henry, his *Psychozoia*, 25 n. 2, 172

Morley, George, Bp of Winchester, his friendship with Waller, 62, 63, 70; his effect upon Denham, 97, 99; a member of Lord Falkland's club, 62, 115

Motteville, Françoise Bertaut de, her *Memoirs of Anne of Austria* quoted, 113, 117

Muleasses the Turk, by John Mason, quoted as a specimen of the bombast of the romantic school, 28, 29

Mulgrave, Earl of, John Sheffield, his *Essay on Poetry*, 248

Murray, William, 114 n.

Nash, Thomas, 23

Nativity Ode, by John Milton, 40, 172

Newcastle, Duchess of, Margaret Lucas, 113

Norris, John, 209, 210

Nosce Teipsum, of Sir John Davies, the first poem of any length in the four-line heroic stanza, 165

Occleve, Thomas, 138

Oceana, by James Harrington, 26

Ode on the Nativity, by John Milton, 40, 172

Oldham, John, Dryden's eulogy of him explained, 234; the first to write heroic verse in complete couplets, 234; effect of his *Satire upon the Jesuits* upon Dryden's verse, 234 n., 245

On a Girdle, by Waller, 72

Opitz, Martin, his *De Contemptu Linguae Teutonicae*, 16; his style, 16; specimen from his *Zlatna*, 16 n.; his aim and influence, 19, 264

Orrery, Lord, Roger Boyle, 95, 171

Ostade, 17 n.

Otway, Thomas, 137, 245

'Overflow' (term proposed by Austin Dobson to translate the French 'enjambement'), the principle of the structure of romantic poetry, 6, 55

Ovid's Banquet of Sense, by George Chapman, 75

Panegyric on Oliver Cromwell, by Edmund Waller, 162 n., 231

Parini, Giuseppe, his connexion between Italian and English verse, 15

Pastor Fido, by Sir Richard Fanshawe, 118, 131

Pater, Walter, his *Marius the Epicurean*, 207 n.

Patmore, Coventry, 187

Pattison, Mark, his definition of the classical movement, 257

Penshurst, by Ben Jonson, its place among topographical poems, 104

Pepys, Samuel, 244 n.

Phaer, Thomas, employs the triple cadence in his version of the *Æneid*, 187

Pharonnida, by William Chamberlayne, 198—202
Philips, John, pompous language of his *Cyder*, 11 n.; his influence on poetry, 11 n.
Philips, Katharine ('Orinda'), 171, 226
Philotas, tragi-comedy by Samuel Daniel, 102 n.
Poetry, difference between the romantic and classical, 6, 19, 55; examples, 7; periods of precise and of romantic, 8; an art, 9; tumbling rimeless measure of Campion, 10; change from particular to general language, 10, 11, 25; its eclectic character in the time of Donne, 25
Polexander, French romance by Marin le Roy Gomberville, 166 n., 261
Polyolbion, by Michael Drayton, 104
Pope, Alexander, class of poetry identical with, 3; effect of the naturalistic poets on his fame, 4, 177; the culmination of classical poetry, 8, 58, 108, 233, 234, 264, 265; his connexion with the story about Shakespeare and the Davenants, 143, 144; sneers at Cowley, 177 and n.; lately come into favour again, 252
Porter, Endymion, 149, 150
Prior, Matthew, 108
Progress of the Soul, by John Donne, 37
Psyche, by Joseph Beaumont, 172
Psychozoia, by Henry More, 25, 172
Purple Island, by Phineas Fletcher, 26, 34, 38, 159

Quarles, Francis, 26, 138

Rabelais, François, quotation from his *Gargantua*, 46 and n.
Racine, Louis, 21, 101
Radcliffe, Alexander, 190 n.
Ralegh, Sir Walter, 36
Randolph, Thomas, 255
Rebel Scot, The, by John Cleveland, 192 and n. 1
Rich, Lady Anne, passage from Sidney Godolphin's verses on her death, 110
Rimed plays, 253
Rival Friends, by Peter Hausted, 116
Rival Ladies, by John Dryden, 54, 95
Rochester, Earl of, John Wilmot, 245
Roscommon, Earl of, Wentworth Dillon, quotation from Waller's epistle to him, 3 n., 245; imitates Milton in his preference for blank verse, 248, 252 n. 1
Rossetti, Dante Gabriel, 20
Rotrou, Jean de, 101
Rupertismus, quotation from John Cleveland's, 186
Rymer, Thomas, writes Waller's epitaph, 51, 52 n.; passage from his *Elegy* on him, 239 n.

Sacharissa, see Lady Dorothy Sidney
Saintsbury, George, his note on *Tyr et Sidon*, 102
Sandys, George, 255, 269, 271
Satire upon the Jesuits, by John Oldham, 234 n.
Selden, John, denounced as a conspirator by Waller, 123
Seneca, style of his tragedies, 102 and n.
Senses' Festival, by John Cleveland, 185

Settle, Elkanah, passage from his *Empress of Marocco*, 252 and n. 2
Shaftesbury, Ashley Cooper, first Earl of, his exaggerated diction, 12
Shakespeare, William, state of English poetry at his death, 3—41 passim; not always clear in metaphor, 12, 13; referred to, 17, 23, 24, 27, 29, 48, 76, 137, 170, 245, 249, 254, 255; the legend that he was the actual father of William Davenant, 141—145; glides sometimes into the triple cadence, 187; feeling of reserve due in reading some of his *Sonnets*, 217
Shelley, Percy Bysshe, 178
Sherburne, Edward, 209 n. 1
Shirley, James, 100, 119, 121; attends his patron, Queen Henrietta Maria, during the Exile, 113, 118
Sidney, Lady Dorothy, Waller's 'Sacharissa,' 63—73, 76—79
„ Lady Lucy, Waller's letter to her on Sacharissa's marriage, 77
„ Sir Philip, 36, 64, 145; his *Arcadia*, 25, 26, 75
Siege of Rhodes, by William Davenant, 168, 169, 242 n.
Sleep and Poetry, quotation from John Keats', 4, 5
Somerville, William, praises Denham in his poem *The Chace*, 108 n. 2
Song to a Rose, by Waller, 70
Song-writing, English, 72; Dryden's songs, 258, 259
Sonnets, of Philip Ayres, 211; of William Shakespeare, 217
Sophy, The, by Sir John Denham, 96, 99—103

Southey, Robert, his position analogous to that of William Davenant, 155—158
Spain, character of, its literature, 177
Spence, Joseph, 264
Spencer, Henry, Earl of Sunderland, marries Lady Dorothy Sidney, 'Sacharissa,' 76; killed at the battle of Newbury, 77
Spenser, Edmund, 17, 19, 24, 27, 48, 169, 170, 249, 254
Sprat, Thomas (Bishop of Rochester), associated with Dryden in his *Heroic Stanzas*, 228 n.
Square Cap, a Cambridge poem by John Cleveland, 190
St Amant, Marc Antoine Gérard, question of his influence on English poetry, 21, 119
St Evremond, Charles, his epigram on Waller, 240 n.
Stanley, Thomas, 203—209
Stanza, the four-line heroic, the chief poems written in it, and its character, 164—166
Starter, Dutch poet, his relation to Thomas Dekker, 17
Stjernhjelm, Georg, first modern Swedish poet, 16
Suckling, Sir John, 22, 59, 150, 151 n., 208
Sunderland, Earl of, see Spencer, Henry
Swinburne, A. C., 178

Taylor, John, the Water poet, 56
„ Sir Henry, 157
Technogamia, by Barton Holiday, 123
Teutonic nations, state of poetry at the close of the sixteenth century among, 15—21

Thalaba, by Robert Southey, 158
Thealma and Clearchus, its disputed authorship, 209 n. 2
To the King on his Navy, passage from Waller's, 55 and n.
Topographical poetry, 104
Tourneur, Cyril, 30—32
Transformed Metamorphosis, by Cyril Tourneur, 31, 32
Translating, Denham's *Essay on the art of*, 98, 99, 272—274
Tyr et Sidon, a French romantic tragedy of the seventeenth century, 102

Upon his Majesty's repairing of Paul's, by Edmund Waller, 79—82

Vaughan, Henry, the Silurist, the last of George Herbert's sacred school of Cambridge poets, 209
Vigil of Venus, by Thomas Stanley, 207
Voltaire, 166
Vondel, Justus vanden, in relation to John Milton, 17; his influence on Dutch poetry, 17, 18

Waller, Edmund, his family, birth, and early life (1605—1621), 48—51; in 1621, member of Parliament for Amersham, 51; member for Chipping Wycombe in Charles I.'s first Parliament (August, 1625), 59; and in the second (Feb. 1626), 60; for Amersham in the third (March, 1628), 60; in 1627 marries Ann Banks, and (1628) retires to Beaconsfield, 60, 61; 1629, his wife dies at Hallbarn, 63; Sacharissa, and the poems addressed to her, 63—73, 76—79; his political career till his banishment (1643), 82—91; 1641, impeaches Sir Francis Crawley on the ship-money question, 84; 1642, quits the 'Root and Branch' party, 84; joins the King, plots against Parliament, his arrest, and narrow escape, 87—91; his life in France during his exile (1643—1653): meets the Royalist Exiles, 117, 122; joined by Evelyn on a tour in Italy, 125—128; 1653, Cromwell allows him to return to, 129, 229, 231; his life at Court after the Restoration (1660—1687), 232—242:
his description of the style of Horace, 3 n.; his purification of verse, 14; his use and treatment of the couplet, 20, 55, 58, 59, 70, 104, 140, 200, 233, 234; question of French influence upon him, 21, 119; the opinion of him expressed in the *Biographia Britannica* (1766), 45; his relations with Dryden, 54, 95, 153, 228 n.; his influence and its reasons, 56, 69, 82, 95, 102, 162, 182—184, 245, 264, 265; his relations with George Morley, 62, 63, 70; his *Battle of the Summer Islands*, 65, 73—76, 150; *Upon his Majesty's repairing of Paul's*, 79—81; his connection with Denham, 63, 79, 80, 96, 102, 105, 120, 140, 156, 177, 183, 219, 228; with Sidney Godolphin, 109, 110, 269; editions of his poems, 124 and n.; his *Panegyric* on Cromwell, 129, 231, 232; Dave-

nant's estimate of his poetry, 150; his relations with Cowley, 171, 174, 177; his use of the triple cadence, 187—189; Wild's eulogy of him, 193, 194; his *Divine Love*, 240, 241; Saint Evremond's epigram on him, 240 n.; rewrites the *Maid's Tragedy* in rimed couplets, 247; Bishop Atterbury's criticism of him, 249—251; his letter to Queen Henrietta Maria, 275—277; Preface to his posthumous poems, 278—284; various allusions to him, 22, 39, 40, 47, 98, 108, 118, 119, 121, 152, 168—171, 173, 174, 187, 203, 208, 210, 211, 226, 229

Walsh, William, his advice to Pope, 264

Walton, Izaak, the probable author of *Thealma and Clearchus*, 209 n. 2

Warburton, William, Bishop of Gloucester, his remark on the study of literature, 138, 139

Warner, William, his *Albion's England*, 75

Webb, John, 242 n.

Webster, John, 24, 100, 137

Weeping of the Magdalen, Richard Crashaw's style in, 14 n.

Wild, Robert, 161, 184, 191—197; his *Iter Boreale*, 161, 192, 193; quotation from his verses on the death of Dr Edmund Calamy, 193 n.

Winchelsea, Countess of, Anne Finch, passage from an unpublished poem of, 256

Windsor Forest, by Alexander Pope, prompted by Denham's *Cooper's Hill*, 108

Wood, Anthony à, his picture of Denham as an undergraduate, 96; reference in his writings to Davenant, 142 n. 1; to Thomas Stanley, 204

Wordsworth, William, assists to revolutionize the taste for classical poetry, 4, 220; his ultimate triumph foreseen by Robert Southey, 156

Wren, Sir Christopher, associated with Sir John Denham in architectural work, 243 and n.

Zlatna, specimen from Martin Opitz's, 16 n.